FAMOUS LINERS AND THEIR STORIES

FAMOUS LINERS

AND

THEIR STORIES

ALAN L. CARY

D. APPLETON-CENTURY COMPANY

INCORPORATED

NEW YORK   LONDON

1937

CONTENTS

DUCHESS OF BEDFORD

One of the four sister ships of the Canadian
Pacific line, designed as very luxurious
cabin class liners for the Canadian
trade. They have proved
themselves very useful
and popular ships.

INTRODUCTION

FROM *PRESIDENT LINCOLN* TO *MINNEWASKA*

THE ships detailed in this book include some of the largest vessels on their respective services or trade routes, and are quite as important and interesting in their own particular way, as the Atlantic giants.

The first vessel in order of date included within the range of tonnages which cover the second sixty of the world's largest liners, is the historic *Great Eastern*, Brunel's gigantic failure. Built at Poplar in the year 1857, she was forty years ahead of her time. The combined paddle wheel and screw propeller drive, together with her five masts equipped with sails, seems humorous to us, accustomed as we are to the stream-lined and clear-cut lines of the modern vessels, with their compact, clean, efficient and almost silent machinery.

It is not necessary here to give the complete history of the *Great Eastern* as so much has already been written about her.

It is interesting to note, however, that it was not until 1902 that a larger liner was built, this being the *Celtic*, the first liner to exceed 20,000 tons gross, and the first of the White Star "big four."

Celtic is the second ship in order of date to be included in this book, being the largest ship afloat when built; an improvement on the *Oceanic* of 1898, but not quite so fast. Built by the same builders, Messrs. Harland & Wolff, Ltd., for the White Star Line, the *Oceanic* was of 17,000 tons.

Celtic after twenty-six years' valuable service, came to grief in 1928 by piling herself on the rocks at the entrance of Queenstown Harbour, in a dense fog.

In the following year (1903) the same builders completed the second of the White Star big four, named *Cedric*, of just over 21,000 tons gross, this again being the largest ship of her day, and generally similar to her sister ship. *Cedric* gave valuable service through peace and war, going to the scrappers in 1932.

This year also saw the German record-making *Kaiser Wilhelm II* in service, a fine, four-funnelled vessel of 19,300 tons gross, with a speed of twenty-three knots. This vessel had an eventful career, and in 1914 was interned in the United States, later becoming the armed cruiser *Agamemnon* of the United States Navy, afterwards being run by the United States Line as the *Monticelli*. She was probably the highest powered quadruple expansion engined liner ever built, and was scrapped in 1933.

Minnesota, of 1904, was the first liner of over 20,000 tons gross to be built in the United States, and the largest American merchant ship built in that country until 1928.

During the war, when the Atlantic Transport Line had all their fleet either sunk or engaged on Government work, the International Mercantile Marine Company transferred her to the Atlantic Transport Company of West Virginia, together with those two well-known Pacific liners *Manchuria* and *Mongolia*, these three keeping up the Atlantic Transport Company's New York–England service.

7

A special feature of the *Minnesota* was the longitudinal water-tight bulkhead, which completely divided the hull into two halves, a separate engine-room and boiler-room being on each side of the ship for each propeller. The holds also were divided, and separate cargo hatchways were on each side of the decks. She had good accommodation for one class of passengers. This vessel was replaced in 1922 by the *Minnetonka* and the *Minnewaska*, and in 1926 she was scrapped in Germany.

Another *Minnesota* then came into the Atlantic Transport Line's fleet, this being the *Zealand* of the Red Star Line, which was transferred to the Atlantic Transport Line and renamed *Minnesota*. She, however, was a smaller vessel of about 12,000 tons, with two funnels.

The Cunard Line had built in 1905 their first 20,000-tonners, these being the famous *Carmania* and *Caronia*, a pair of fine, roomy ships of medium speed, built for the secondary service from Liverpool to New York. These sister ships were alike except as to engines. To enable the Cunard directors and engineers to

HANSA

obtain their own data on the running and efficiency of the Parson's steam turbine, before deciding on the type of machinery to be installed in the two projected big ships, they had the best available quadruple expansion steam engines installed in the *Caronia*, and Parson's steam turbines in the *Carmania*. The result was soon found to be in favour of the turbines, as *Carmania* proved herself faster and more efficient than her sister, and afterwards confirmed in the wonderful machinery fitted into the *Lusitania* and *Mauretania*.

The *Carmania* and *Caronia*, coming through the war with added glory, were on many services, finishing up on the London–New York service. They were laid up for some time in Tilbury Docks, and finally sold to the scrappers in 1932.

The next ship in the series came out in 1907, and was the German Lloyd liner *Kronprinzessin Cecilie*, a big passenger carrier of moderate speed. She was a very successful ship on the Bremen–New York service until 1914, when she was interned in the United States, later becoming the *Mount Vernon* of the United States Line.

INTRODUCTION

The Red Star Line had built in 1908, by Harland & Wolff, a big liner named *Lapland*, with a gross tonnage of 18,000 tons. She was the largest ship of the line, and the largest to date to use the port of Antwerp. A big emigrant carrier, she had also good saloon and cabin accommodation.

The next two liners of over 18,000 tons were the Allan Line's biggest pair, *Alsatian* and *Calgarian*, the former better known as the *Empress of France*. This fine pair of ships were the biggest pre-war liners on the Canadian run. Both had an active war history, being sold in 1916 to the Canadian Pacific Railway, with the rest of the Allan Line fleet, the *Calgarian* being lost on war service in 1918.

The *Alsatian* made history during the war by being selected as flagship of the famous 10th Cruiser Squadron. They were an exceedingly fine pair of ships, and were built by the Allan Line to meet the increasing competition by the Canadian Pacific Railway's "Empress" class, and the White Star Line's Dominion ships.

The White Star liner *Ceramic* came out in 1913 from Harland & Wolff's yard at Belfast, a big four-master of 18,500 gross tons, designed for the Australian via Cape Town service of the line. She was later transferred to the Shaw, Savill & Albion Line, and is still that line's largest vessel.

Germany, in 1914, was building at Hamburg a fine 20,000 tonner for the South American trade of the Hamburg–Sud Amerika Line. She was named *Cap Polonio* and was intended to run as consort to the *Cap Trafalgar*, which was sunk after a gun action with the *Carmania* in September, 1914, while both ships were serving as armed merchant cruisers.

Cap Polonio was laid aside during the war uncompleted, but the German naval authorities had her accommodation converted into a naval hospital at Hamburg. After the war she was ceded to Great Britain under the Peace Treaty, and after running for the Shipping Controller under Cunard and P. & O. management, she was sold back to the line, for which she was originally intended, in 1922. The people of Hamburg were overjoyed when the great ship arrived at her home port of Hamburg, wearing the flag of the great line that had had her built. Cheering crowds lined the quay-side to greet her.

Scenes of the greatest enthusiasm were also witnessed when she made her departure from Hamburg on her first trip to South America. So popular was she, that a famous hotel at Pinneberg was renamed Hotel Cap Polonio, in honour of the great ship. The German people saw in her the revival of their hopes in getting back to their lost maritime position.

Cap Polonio was scrapped in 1935, after thirteen years' good service for the great Hamburg Sud-Amerika Line.

In Germany, the Hamburg–Amerika Line had a fine 21,000-ton liner half completed as the war began, she was to have been named *Tirpitz*. The Kaiser, convincing himself of victory, gave orders that the *Tirpitz* should be completed and fitted out as a luxurious steam yacht for the use of himself and his staff when the Allied naval fleets surrendered to him, but alas for his hopes, in 1919 *Tirpitz* which had as yet never been to sea was, under the Peace Treaty of Versailles, handed over to the British Controller of Shipping. After a number of voyages under the Cunard Line management she was sold to the Canadian Pacific Railway Company. Being re-fitted at Liverpool she was re-named *Empress of Australia* as a happy token of respect to the great Continent of the South. She is a lovely ship of 21,861 tons gross, and has had a successful career under the Check flag of the C.P.R., being popular both on regular service and on cruising, having very fine and luxurious accommodation. After some time in service she was found to be a very uneconomical vessel and later was sent to the Clyde to have her quadruple expansion reciprocating engines removed and replaced by Parson's steam turbines. She left the shipyard practically a new vessel and on her steam trials did twenty knots with a greatly reduced fuel cost.

The *München*, a ship of nearly 19,000 tons, was practically completed in Germany and held up in the builders' yard, being finished off early in 1920 and handed over under the Peace Treaty to the British Shipping Controller. She was later sold to the Royal Mail Steam Packet Company, and renamed *Ohio*, then placed on the Company's new North Atlantic service to New York.

When the White Star Line was purchased by the Royal Mail Steam Packet Company, this service was stopped, and the *Ohio* was transferred to the White Star Line and renamed *Albertic* and put on the Canadian service. Afterwards

The Boat Deck of the CARNARVON CASTLE

she did useful work on other services, and some cruising work, finally going to the scrappers in 1934.

In 1920, the great shipping lines commenced to order new tonnage to make good their tremendous war losses, and to cope with the post-war emigration, and the expansion of trade which was created by the world-wide demand for goods.

The Cunard Line commenced a series of fine twenty thousand ton liners with the *Scythia* of 1920, a splendid twin screw turbine-driven ship, and a modern repetition of the famous *Carmania*.

In Germany, two ships which had been ordered by the Hamburg–Amerika Line, named *William O'Swald* and *Johann Heinrich Burchard*, were completed and handed over by the German Authorities to Holland, in recompense for shipping lost during the submarine campaign. The Allies protested, and finally the two vessels were transferred to the United States and renamed *Resolute* and *Reliance*, and run by The United American Line, which was running in conjunction with the Hamburg–Amerika Line between New York and Hamburg. Later they were sold to the Hamburg–Amerika Line, being that line's first Atlantic liners after the war.

The *Resolute* was sold to Italy in 1935 for use as a troop transport.

Italy came in as a builder of big ships in the year 1921 by having the *Guilio Cesare* built by Swan, Hunter & Wigham Richardson, Ltd., at Newcastle. This was Italy's first liner to exceed 21,000 tons. The *Guilio Cesare* is a fine ship, and later, a sister ship, the *Duilio*, was built.

The second post-war Cunarder of the 20,000 tons class came out in 1921 and was named *Samaria*, a similar vessel to her sister.

The Union Castle Mail S.S. Company, Ltd., built their first post-war liner in 1921, by Harland & Wolff, named *Arundel Castle*. She was the first of a pair of 19,000 ton liners, the largest at that time built for the South African service. The second, named *Windsor Castle*, came out in 1922 from the same builders. The year 1922 saw also the third of the Cunard 20,000 tonners come out, the *Laconia*, a sister ship to the previous two, and a very popular cruising vessel she proved to be.

The first of the two big ships for the Atlantic Transport Line, *Minnewaska*, made her debut in 1923. Her sister, *Minnetonka*, of slightly greater tonnage, came out in 1924.

Minnewaska was of 21,761 gross tons, and the two sister ships were the largest the company ever had. Like her sister, she was transferred to the Red Star Line in 1932, and was finally scrapped in 1934 when the International Mercantile Marine Company decided to rid themselves of their European lines and ships.

The *Franconia*, the popular liner of the Cunard Line, came out also in 1923; the P. & O. Steam Navigation Company bringing out two fine ships this year for their London–Bombay Mail and Australian service. These were the splendid *Maloja* and *Mooltan* of nearly 21,000 tons gross, and were the largest vessels built for the line, to date. The Hamburg–Amerika Line making financial recovery, brought out two new ships in the same year, one being the *Albert Ballin*, named after the late head of the Company, who for so many years had done so much in building up the line that in 1914 was the largest shipping line in the world under one house-flag. The second ship received the historic and patriotic name *Deutschland*.

The Pacific fleet of the Canadian Pacific Line requiring new tonnage, the *Empress of Canada* was built by Fairfield's of Glasgow this same year, and placed in service in 1923, the largest vessel to date on the Pacific Ocean, she being of 21,500 tons gross.

Italy built a fine pair of ships of over 18,000 tons each, named *Conte Verde* and *Conte Rosso*, in 1922 and 1923. They are the largest ships constructed as yet for the Lloyd Triestino Line of Trieste, and are generally employed on the Far Eastern service of the combined Italia Line Services with the motor vessel *Victoria*, which, prior to the coming out of the P. & O. liner *Strathmore*, was the fastest vessel in that trade.

The Orient Line of London, having lost most of their pre-war fleet during the war, had been running their services with three ex-German ships and the survivors of their own fleet. In 1924 they commenced their new programme by having built the first of their present fine 20,000 tonners, which are so popular on the Australian trade. This was the *Orama*, built by Vickers, Ltd., at Barrow, the previous ship of the same name having been torpedoed in 1917, after two years of escort work as an auxiliary cruiser. Previously she had assisted in the destruction of Admiral Von Spee's fleet, being at the final episode on that historic naval occasion when the last of the gallant Admiral's vessels, the *Dresden*, was rounded up.

France's great trans-Atlantic company, Cie. Generale Transatlantique, also in 1924 added a big cabin class liner to its fleet, the *De Grasse*, of 18,400 tons gross, usually employed on the West Indies trade.

The last of the Cunard fine 20,000 tonners, the *Carinthia*, one of the most popular liners in the world of her size, went into service in 1925, and is generally similar to her sister ships.

In 1925 two more of the Orient Line's 20,000 tonners came out, the *Otranto* and the *Oronsay*, the former by Vickers, Ltd., and the *Oronsay* by John Brown. They were in keeping with the high standard and traditions of this famous line. The former bears a name honoured in the history of the line, the previous *Otranto*, like the *Orama*, was an auxiliary cruiser during the war, being attached to

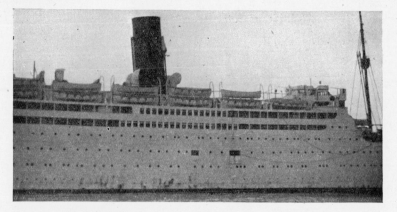

CARINTHIA *one of the Cunard White Star* 20,000 *tonners*

Admiral Craddock's ill-fated squadron, and was fortunate in escaping from the disastrous action at Coronel.

The only vessel in our list for 1924 is the Union Castle Line's first motor ship, *Carnarvon Castle*, of 20,000 tons gross, also being the first liner of the line to exceed the 20,000 tons mark. Built by Harland & Wolff, she is a fine, luxurious ship, and, with the later motor ships, have been very popular on the South African run.

Furness, Withy & Co., Ltd., owners of the Bermuda & West Indies S.S. Company, had a fine motor ship built by Workman, Clarke & Co., at Belfast. The *Bermuda* was the largest liner yet to be built for this short voyage, being of nearly 20,000 tons. Early in her career she was unfortunately damaged by fire when in Bermuda, and on being taken to Belfast for repairs she again had a fire on board, becoming a total loss. She was replaced by the *Queen of Bermuda* in 1933, the Cunard liner *Franconia* being chartered meanwhile to take the place of the ill-fated *Bermuda*.

The *Laurentic* was built also in 1927 for the White Star Line by Harland & Wolff. A fine cabin class liner of nearly 19,000 tons gross, she was designed for the Canadian trade, but has been used on several services, also on cruising work. She was laid up at the end of the 1935 season and in 1936 was commissioned as a troopship.

The year 1928 saw the new turbo-electric drive applied for the first time to passenger liners. The American S.S. Corporation, a branch of the International Mercantile Marine Company of New York, had two 18,000 ton vessels built with this new drive. These fine ships are employed on the New York–California coastal run via the Panama Canal. They were named *Virginia* and *California*, and in 1929 a third was built named *Pennsylvania*.

Sweden this same year (1928) came into the list of big ship owners by putting into service the beautiful motor ship *Kungsholm*, built in Germany for the Swedish–America Line. She is consort to the *Drottingholm* which was formerly the *Virginian* of the Allan Line, one of the two first turbine liners ever built.

In Great Britain, the Canadian Pacific Line astonished the shipping world by bringing out three 20,000 ton cabin class liners, fitted out with a degree of luxury never before attempted in cabin liners. These were the *Duchess of Bedford*, *Duchess of Atholl* and *Duchess of Richmond*. People who thought they knew the passenger trade prophesied a failure for the cabin class ship, but they did not realise the changes that were taking place. After Prince George travelled in one on his return from duty on the China station their popularity was assured.

A year later, a fourth ship, the *Duchess of York*, joined the three sisters, and the four fine ships maintain the Liverpool–Canadian weekly service. They all have, too, proved themselves very acceptable as cruising ships, and have a large following which fully justifies the enterprise of the Company. This type of ship is a step nearer to the great one-class liner of the future, carrying upwards of 10,000 passengers.

The Orient Line's fourth of their 20,000 ton series came from the Barrow yard of Vickers Armstrong, Ltd., in 1928, this vessel being named *Orford*, a worthy sister to the previous vessels.

Britain's first turbo-electric liner, the famous and luxurious *Viceroy of India*, was built by Alex. Stephen & Sons at Glasgow for the Peninsular and Oriental Steam Navigation Company. The beautiful ship, equipped with every refinement, has, ever since, been the most popular ship on the London–Bombay run. Her splendid and artistic scheme of decoration was designed by the late Miss Mackay, daughter of the late Lord Inchcape, who shortly afterwards lost her life in an attempt to fly the Atlantic. The *Viceroy of India* has proved herself a wonderful, trouble-free and valuable vessel, being the hardest worked ship of the line. She is also a great favourite for luxury cruises.

The Orient Line's fifth 20,000 tonner came out also in the same year, *Orontes* being the name of this fine ship, joining her sisters on the London–Australia via Suez and Ceylon route.

The Nederland Steamship Company nearly reached the 20,000 ton mark in 1930 when they added to their fleet the two 19,000 ton motor ships, *Marnix Van Sint Aldegonde* and *Johan Van Oldenbarnevelt*, a fine pair with beautiful accommodation designed for the Far East trade. They are the largest ships the line has yet owned, and since their inception have been kept busily engaged.

The Union Castle Line, always keeping up with the times, added a pair of splendid motor ships to their mail fleet in 1930, each of over 20,000 tons gross.

They were named *Warwick Castle* and *Winchester Castle*, generally similar to the *Carnarvon Castle* but with some improvements. They were, like the *Carnarvon Castle*, built by Harland & Wolff at Belfast.

Italy, in 1932 and 1933, built a pair of motor vessels of 19,500 tons gross, named *Neptunia* and *Oceania*, owned by the Cosulich branch of the Italia Line. They were designed for the South American run; two motor engines being geared to each of the two propeller shafts.

The years 1932, 1933 and 1934 saw no new British liners within the tonnage limit of this book, and the remainder of the sixty ships include the three fine Matson liners, *Lurline*, *Monterey* and *Mariposa*, built for the San Francisco, Honolulu, Hawaii and Australian Services of this famous and old established Californian line.

They are twin screw turbine steamers, each of just over 18,500 tons, with

The Dutch Liner JOHAN VAN OLDENBARNEVELT

very luxurious and excellent passenger accommodation which has brought all the luxury and the amenities of the Atlantic liners to the Pacific.

Germany in 1935 brought out her first turbine-electric liner, the *Scharnhorst*, followed by a sister ship, except as to drive, the *Gneisenau*, and another sister ship, except as to hull form, named the *Potsdam*. All three of these fine ships were intended to be turbo-electric driven, but to ease the unemployment situation at the shipyards the *Gneisenau* was given reduction geared turbine drive.

These three fine ships have enabled the Norddeutscher Lloyd to again take their place in the Far Eastern trades.

Separate and full details of each ship will be found in the following pages together with illustrations and scale silhouettes, and in the latter part of the book are some interesting histories of famous British steamship lines and their fleets.

I again express my thanks for the kind assistance given me by the various Shipping Companies, British, American and European, and to the help derived from the Shipping periodicals.

FAMOUS LINERS AND THEIR STORIES

EXPLANATIONS OF ABBREVIATIONS
USED IN TEXT

Gross or register tonnage .	Cubic feet capacity of all enclosed space divided by 100.
Nat. & Port . . .	Country and port of registry.
Length	Length o.a.—overall, b.p.—between perpendiculars.
Depth	Depth of vessel. Drt. draught at normal load.
Nor. Spd. . . .	Normal service speed.
Knots	1 nautical mile per hour, or 1·1515 land miles per hour.
Dimensions . . .	Dimensions of hull.
S.H.P.	Shaft horse-power.
B.H.P.	Brake horse-power.
I.H.P.	Indicated horse-power.
F.D.	Forced draught to furnaces.
S.H.	Super heated steam to temperature given.
Trip. ex. . . .	Triple expansion, reciprocating steam engines.
Quad. ex. . . .	Quadruple expansion, reciprocating steam engines.
Cyls.	Cylinders in reciprocating steam or motor engines.
S.A.	Single-acting, applied to Diesel motor engines.
D.A.	Double-acting, applied to Diesel motor engines.
2 st.	Two-stroke, applied to Diesel motor engines.
4 st.	Four-stroke, applied to Diesel motor engines.

No. 1. EMPRESS OF AUSTRALIA. 1914

(Ex. Empress of China, Ex. Tirpitz)

OWNERS:	Canadian Pacific S.S., Ltd.
SERVICE:	Southampton–Quebec, and Cruising.
NAT. & PORT:	British. London.
BUILDERS:	Akt. Ges. Vulcan, Bredow, Stettin, Germany, 1914.
TONNAGE:	21,861 tons gross.
DIMENSIONS:	615 ft. lg. oa., 589½ ft. lg. b.p. x 75 ft. beam x 42 ft. depth. 5 decks
ENGINES:	Two sets steam turbines, 20,000 s.h.p. By Fairfield Co., Glasgow Twin screw. Normal speed 19 knots.
BOILERS:	6 D.E. and 6 S.E. boilers, 220 lbs. stm. pr. 600 deg. S.H. Oil fuel, F.D
PAINTWORK:	Hull white with blue band and green boot-topping, upperwork white, funnels buff.
COMPLEMENT:	400 1st class, 150 tourist, 635 3rd class. 520 officers and crew.

Ex Hamburg–Amerika Line.

Dining hall is in French Regency style, spacious lounge in Empire style with dance floor. Writing room is Louis XVI with tinted walls and mahogany furniture, smoke room is à la Louis XIV with oak panelled walls. Swimming pool and gymnasium are also very fine and well equipped.

She was commenced at Stettin in 1914, but building was held up during war in 1916, however, the Kaiser ordered her to be completed as a royal yacht in which he would receive the allied naval fleets when they surrendered.

1919. She was ceded to Great Britain under the Peace Treaty and made her first trip from Hamburg to Hull.

1922. Sold by Shipping Controller to the Canadian Pacific Railway. Refitted by John Brown & Co., Ltd., Clydebank.

1925. The original quadruple expansion reciprocating engines were removed and replaced by Fairfields, Glasgow, with Parson's steam turbines, and converted for oil firing.

On trials did average speed of 20·3 knots.

Oil fuel consumed 150 tons per day.

Very popular cruising ship. In Jan., 1935, left Southampton on extended cruise, taking mails, etc., to the lonely Pacific Isle of Tristan de Cunha.

1935, April 4th. Her commander, Capt. E. Griffiths, brought her into Southampton on his last voyage before retiring after having navigated every big ship in the C.P.R. fleet and having forty-eight years at sea, during which he has sailed round the world three times and crossed the Atlantic 700 times.

EMPRESS OF AUSTRALIA

No. 2. MINNEWASKA. 1923

OWNERS:	The Atlantic Transport Line, London.
SERVICE:	London–New York.
NAT. & PORT:	British. London.
BUILDERS:	Messrs. Harland & Wolff, Ltd., Belfast, 1923.
TONNAGE:	21,716 tons gross.
DIMENSIONS:	601 ft. lg. x 80 ft. beam x 49 ft. depth. 3 decks.
ENGINES:	Two sets of Brown-Curtis type steam turbines. Sin. red. geared 15,000 s.h.p. Twin screw. Normal speed 16½ knots.
BOILERS:	12 water tube boilers. Oil fuel, consumption 165 tons per day.
PAINTWORK:	Hull black with red band, boot-topping red, upper works white funnel red with black top.
COMPLEMENT:	1st class only, 368 passengers.

Previous ship of same name sunk in war by enemy action.

With sister ship, *Minnetonka*, had the largest cargo capacity of any ships buil to date, 20,000 tons, cost £1,175,000. Were the largest ships to use Londo docks prior to the P. & O. "Strath" ships.

1923, Sept. 1st. Maiden voyage London to New York. Capt. T. F. Gate

1924, May. Capt. Gates transferred to *Minnetonka*, Capt. F. H. Claret.

1931. Laid up at Southend.

1932. Transferred to Red Star Line, Antwerp to New York Service. Sh was painted in Red Star colours.

1933. Laid up at Antwerp.

1934. Along with her sister ship sold to Messrs Douglas & Ramsey, ship breakers, for £35,000. Broken up.

Never before have such splendid and comparatively new vessels been sent t the scrapper's yard.

MINNEWASKA

[*By courtesy of Atlantic Transport Line*

No. 3. GUILIO CESARE. 1923

OWNERS: Italia Line (Navigazione Generale Italiana).
SERVICE: Italy–South Africa.
NAT. & PORT: Italian. Genoa.
BUILDERS: Swan, Hunter & Wigham Richardson, Ltd., Newcastle-on-Tyne, 1923.
TONNAGE: 21,657 tons gross.
DIMENSIONS: 636 ft. lg. oa. x 76·15 ft. beam x 46·3 ft. depth. 4 decks.
ENGINES: 4 sets of steam turbines. 21,800 s.h.p. Quad. screw. Normal speed
               19 knots.
BOILERS: 6 D.E. and 4 S.E. boilers, 220 lbs. stm. pr. By Wallsend Slipway &
               Engineering Co., Ltd., Newcastle.
PAINTWORK: White hull and upper works, boot-topping green, funnels white with
               red and black tops and narrow green band.

Sister ship *Duilio.* Very handsome ships, carrying 1st, 2nd and tourist class
passengers; a special feature is the "Club" situated on the boat-deck, with its
cosy bar; the saloon dining room is especially beautiful. There are also lovely
galleries, ballroom, etc. Second class accommodation is also very fine and is
situated amidships. "Talkie" apparatus and a long-distance wireless telephone
are also fitted. The tourist class accommodation situated astern has several
fine public rooms and tourist passengers share an open air swimming pool with
the 2nd class.

1933, Nov. Reconditioned for Mediterranean–South Africa Service.

1935. German steamship *Barenfels* came into collision with her off Gibraltar
Bay and the German ship was placed under arrest.

GUILIO CESARE

No. 4. EMPRESS OF CANADA. 1920

Owners:	Canadian Pacific S.S. Ltd.
Service:	Vancouver–Tokio, Shanghai and Hong Kong.
Nat. & Port:	British. Vancouver, B.C.
Builders:	Fairfield Co., Ltd., Glasgow, 1920.
Tonnage:	21,517 tons gross.
Dimensions:	653 ft. lg. oa., 627 ft. lg. b.p. x 78 ft. beam x 42 ft. depth. 4 decks.
Engines:	2 sets of steam turbines. 26,000 s.h.p. Twin screw. Normal speed 20 knots.
Boilers:	8 D.E. and 4 S.E. boilers, 210 lbs. stm. pr. 650 deg. S.H. Oil fuel, consumes 220 tons of oil per day.
Paintwork:	White hull with blue band and green boot-topping, white upper works, buff funnels.
Complement:	488 1st, 106 2nd, 238 intermediate, 926 3rd class. Officers and crew 500.

Cost £1,700,000.

A beautiful ship on the same lines as the *Empress of Japan* only smaller, with the usual Canadian Pacific high standard of accommodation. Very popular on the Pacific run.

1920. Launched.

1923. Raced U.S. liner *President Jackson* across Pacific and won by 12 hours. Record passage from Yokohama to Vancouver 8 days 10 hours 53 mins.

1933, Sept. 18th. Captain reported her leaking and returned to Yokohama for dry docking.

EMPRESS OF CANADA

[By courtesy of Canadian Pacific Line

No. 5. HANSA. 1923

(Ex. Albert Ballin)

OWNERS: Hamburg–Amerika Line.

SERVICE: Hamburg–New York.

NAT. & PORT: German. Hamburg.

BUILDERS: Blohm & Voss, Kommandit Ges auf Aktien, Hamburg, 1923.

TONNAGE: 21,131 tons gross.

DIMENSIONS: 645 ft. lg. oa. x 75 ft. beam x 44·7 ft. depth. 4 decks.

ENGINES: 8 steam turbines, 20,000 s.h.p. Twin screw. Normal speed 20 knots.

BOILERS: 4 D.E. and 4 S.E. boilers, 400 lbs. stm. pr.

PAINTWORK: Hull black, boot-topping red, upper works white, funnels buff with red, white and black tops.

COMPLEMENT: 966 passengers in 1st, tourist and 3rd classes. 422 officers and crew.

The first of the "Ballin" class of the line, named after Herr Albert Ballin, late head of the Company, who died in 1918. Sister ship *Deutschland,* and very similar in appearance to the other ships of the class only that the two earlier ones *Albert Ballin* and *Deutschland* have four masts while the two later ones have only two. Their appointments are on the same lavish scale that has always been a feature of the line. The four ships of this class maintain a regular weekly service between Hamburg and New York, one vessel leaving each port every Thursday, and they take seven days on the voyage. They are very popular both with the German and American travelling public, who prefer steadiness and comfort to speed.

1929-30. With the *Deutschland* was re-boilered and re-engined, the H.P. being increased from 19,000 to 28,000 and the speed raised from 16 knots to 20 knots.

1934. Lengthened and H.P. reduced to 20,000.

1936, Jan. Renamed *Hansa*.

HANSA

[By courtesy of the Hamburg-Amerika Line

No. 6. CEDRIC. 1903

OWNERS: White Star Line.
SERVICE: Liverpool–New York.
NAT. & PORT: British. Liverpool.
BUILDERS: Messrs. Harland & Wolff, Ltd., Belfast, 1903.
TONNAGE: 21,073 tons gross.
DIMENSIONS: 681 ft. lg. oa. x 73 ft. beam x 44 ft. depth. 5 decks.
ENGINES: 2 quad. exp. 4 cyl. recip. engines, 14,000 s.h.p. Twin screw. Normal
               speed 17 knots.
PAINTWORK: Black hull with gold line, red boot-topping, white upper works, buff
               funnels with black tops.
COMPLEMENT: 1,223 passengers, 486 officers and crew.

Was largest ship built to date. Second of the White Star "big four." Very
comfortable and steady ship, exceedingly popular in her day and notable for her
great economy.

1902, Aug. 21st. Launched.

1928. Refitted and converted to cabin class, with accommodation for 1,223
passengers and 486 officers and crew.

1932, Feb. Sold to shipbreakers.

CEDRIC

[By courtesy of Cunard White Star Line

No. 7. DEUTSCHLAND. 1923

OWNERS:	Hamburg-Amerika Line.
SERVICE:	Hamburg–New York.
NAT. & PORT:	German. Hamburg.
BUILDERS:	Blohm & Voss, Kommandit Ges auf Aktien, Hamburg, 1923.
TONNAGE:	21,046 tons gross.
DIMENSIONS:	645 ft. lg. oa. x 72.25 ft. beam x 41.9 ft. depth. 4 decks.
ENGINES:	8 steam turbines, 28,000 s.h.p. Twin screw. Normal speed, 20 knots.
BOILERS:	4 D.E. and 4 S.E. boilers, stm. pr. 400 lbs.
PAINTWORK:	Hull black, boot-topping red, upper works white, funnels buff with red, white and black tops.
COMPLEMENT:	976 passengers in 1st, tourist and 3rd class. 422 officers and crew.

She is the fourth in size of the "Ballin" class, and was named after her famous predecessor the *Deutschland* of 1900, which had a tonnage of 16,502 tons gross, and which held the Atlantic record for some years with a speed of 23.51 knots; she was later renamed *Victoria Luise* and was converted to a cruising yacht and was broken up in 1925. The present ship with her three sisters, while not record makers either in size or speed, are entirely modern and have the appearance of efficient utility.

1930, March 10th. When she was docking at Pier 84, North River, New York, she was blown against the pier in a gale and had starboard plating indented.

1933, Nov. 11th. Dry docked in New York after collision in New York bay with United States steamer *Munargo*, 6,484 tons. Bows of *Deutschland* damaged six feet above waterline.

1935, August 7th. Scores of police guarded her sailing from New York following the demonstrations which occurred when the *Bremen* sailed; the *Deutschland* did not however fly the Swastika flag. Departure made without disturbance.

DEUTSCHLAND

[By courtesy of the Hamburg-Amerika Line

No. 8. CAP POLONIO. 1914

OWNERS:	Die Hamburg-Sudamerikanische Dampfshifffahrts Gesellschaft. The Hamburg South American Steamship Company.
SERVICE:	Hamburg–South American Ports.
NAT. & PORT:	German. Hamburg.
BUILDERS:	Herrn Blohm & Voss, Hamburg, 1914.
TONNAGE:	21,011 tons gross, 9,951 tons net.
DIMENSIONS:	637·5 ft. lg. o.a. x 72·3 ft. beam x 39 ft. depth. 5 pass. decks.
ENGINES:	Two 4 cyl. Quad. exp. recip. engines and 1 low pressure turbine, 18,000 s.h.p. Triple screw. Normal speed, 18 knots.
PAINTWORK:	Hull black, upper works white, boot-topping red, funnels white with red tops.
COMPLEMENT:	1,100 passengers.

A similar ship but smaller than the *Cap Arcona*, but larger than her predecessor the *Cap Trafalgar*. A very elegant and well proportioned ship, her three great funnels, straight stem and counter stern giving her a fine graceful appearance.

She would have been the largest ship on the South American route had she been able to take her allotted place in 1914. She was ordered by the Hamburg–Sud–Amerika Company late in 1913 in extension of their policy of providing an express service with ships of the "Cap" class. Her name was taken from the Cape which is between the borders of Brazil and the mouth of the La Plata river, on the coast of Uruguay.

1914, March. Launched by Herrn. Blohm & Voss at Hamburg.

1914, August. The still uncompleted ship was, on the outbreak of war, hurriedly fitted out as a hospital ship on the orders of the German Naval Authorities and commissioned as H.S. *Vineto*.

1919. By the Peace Treaty of Versailles she was ceded to Great Britain, and handed over to the British Shipping Controller, who placed her under the management of the P. & O. S.N. Company, and she was mainly employed on transporting home Indian and African troops.

1921, July. The Hamburg South American Company bought her back, to place her on originally intended service, to the great satisfaction of the Hamburg and German people generally; on her arrival at Hamburg she received a great welcome. She was taken to her builders where she received a complete re-fit and on the

7th April, 1922, she commenced her first trip to South America under her own flag. Commanded by Commodore Rolin, her departure was the scene of great enthusiasm and rejoicing and the eyes of all the German people were on her. Thousands of people lined the banks of the Elbe and wildly cheered her on her way down to the sea. Her initial voyage was a great success and she became a very popular ship on both sides of the Atlantic.

CAP POLONIO

1922, Dec. She commenced a series of cruises from South American ports, and the accommodation was quickly sold out. In 1923 she did a further three such cruises in between her regular voyages.

1926. She did a special 80-day cruise from South America via Spain, Edinboro, Norway, Sweden to Leningrad.

1931. Owing to the economic crisis she was laid up at Waltershaven on the River Elbe.

1935, June. A great ship came to her end by being sold to scrappers for breaking up. The ship and name will long live in German hearts and the advent of the new Flagship of the fleet, *Cap Arcona*, has not erased the memory of this famous ship. So popular was she in Hamburg that the owners of the Hotel Stad Hamburg on the Rosenstadt at Pinneburg, a popular resort of the Hamburgers, have changed the name of the hotel to Cap Polonio.

No. 9. MOOLTAN. 1923

OWNERS:	The Peninsular & Oriental Steam Navigation Co.
SERVICE:	London–India–China–Australia mail and passenger service.
NAT. & PORT:	British. Belfast.
BUILDERS:	Messrs. Harland & Wolff, Ltd., Belfast, 1923.
TONNAGE:	20,952 tons gross.
DIMENSIONS:	600·5 ft. lg. b.p. x 73·5 ft. beam x 48·5 ft. depth. 5 decks.
ENGINES:	2 Quad. exp. 4 cyl. recip. steam engines. 15,300 s.h.p. Inverted direct acting, balanced to eliminate vibration. Twin screw. Normal speed 17½ knots.
BOILERS:	6 D.E. and 2 S.E. boilers, 215 lbs. stm. pr. Oil fuel.
PAINTWORK:	Black hull with white line, red boot-topping, stone upper works, black funnels.
COMPLEMENT:	327 1st and 329 2nd class.

With her sister ship marked a new phase in the development of the P. & O. fleet; largest ships, when put in service, on Indian and Australian trade, a notable feature being the excellence of the 2nd class accommodation.

1929. Had exhaust turbine, Bauer-Wach system, fitted.

1933. Carried Australian Test team home.

1934, Dec. Underwent extensive re-fit at Tilbury, passenger accommodation brought up to latest standards.

1936, April. Captain F. E. French of the *Corfu* appointed commander.

[*By courtesy of the P. & O. Line*

MOOLTAN

No. 10. CELTIC. 1901

OWNERS: White Star Line.

SERVICE: Liverpool–New York.

NAT. & PORT: British. Liverpool.

BUILDERS: Messrs. Harland & Wolff, Ltd., Belfast, 1901.

TONNAGE: 20,904 tons gross.

DIMENSIONS: 681 ft. lg. oa. x 75 ft. beam. x 44·7 ft. depth. 4 decks.

ENGINES: 2 Quad. exp. 4 cyl. steam engines, 14,000 s.h.p. Twin screw. Norma speed 17 knots.

PAINTWORK: Black hull with gold line, white upper works, buff funnels with blac tops.

COMPLEMENT: 347 1st class, 260 2nd class, 2,342 3rd class.

The first of the White Star Line's "big four."

Largest ship afloat to date. First liner to exceed 20,000 tons.

Built on White Star Line's policy of spacious, comfortable ships of moderat speed.

1928. Converted to cabin class.

1928. Went aground in fog at entrance to Queenstown Harbour, becam total wreck. No casualties.

1933. Owing to dangerous position of wreck the hull was cut up with acetylen blow-pipes.

[By courtesy of Cunard White Star Line

CELTIC

34

OWNERS:	Peninsular & Oriental Steam Navigation Co.
SERVICE:	London–India–China–Australia Mail and Passenger.
NAT. & PORT:	British. Belfast.
BUILDERS:	Messrs. Harland & Wolff, Ltd., Belfast, 1923.
TONNAGE:	20,837 tons gross.
DIMENSIONS:	600·8 ft. lg. b.p. x 73·4 ft. beam x 48·6 ft. depth. 5 decks.
ENGINES:	2 Quad. exp. 4 cyl. recip. engines, 15,300 s.h.p. Inverted direct acting, balanced to eliminate vibration. Twin screw. Normal speed 17½ knots.
BOILERS:	6 D.E. and 2 S.E. boilers, stm. pr. 215 lbs. Oil fuel.
PAINTWORK:	Black hull with white line, red boot-topping, upper works stone, funnels black.
COMPLEMENT:	327 1st and 329 2nd class.

The luxurious public rooms, in keeping with the usual high standard of the, line, are beautiful and lofty. All cabins are porthole cabins both in the 1st and 2nd classes. The dining saloon, seating 330 persons, is plainly but pleasantly panelled in Georgian style, finished throughout in ivory white. The reading and music saloon is in Louis XVI style with large french windows. Sister ship *Mooltan.*

1929. Had exhaust turbine fitted, Bauer-Wach system.

1933, June. Was ashore for two hours on Australian coast but was refloated undamaged.

1934, Oct. Owners gave Mrs. Don Bradman a free passage in her when Don Bradman was taken ill in England.

1934, Nov. 24th. Left Tilbury with one of the heaviest cargoes which had left Tilbury for some time, for Australian ports.

1936, April. Captain J. B. Browning, commander and Vice-Commodore of the P. & O. fleet, appointed Commodore in succession to Captain E. J. Thornton, retired.

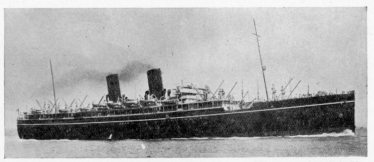

[By courtesy of P. & O. Line

MALOJA

No. 12. MINNESOTA. 1904

OWNERS: Great Northern Steamship Company.
SERVICE: New York–London. 1914-1918.
NAT. & PORT: United States. New York.
BUILDERS: Eastern Ship Building Co., New London, Conn., U.S., 1904.
TONNAGE: 20,708 tons gross.
DIMENSIONS: 622 ft. lg. oa. x 73½ ft. beam x 41½ ft. depth. Drt. 38 ft. 5 decks.
ENGINES: 2 triple exp., 3 cyl. recip. engines, 14,000 s.h.p. Twin screw. Norma
              speed 13 knots.
BOILERS: 16 water tube. Oil fuel.
PAINTWORK: Black hull with yellow band, white upper works, funnel red with black
              top.

The largest merchant vessel built in the United States for over twenty years
afterwards. The only ship built with the hull entirely divided longitudinally
by watertight bulkheads, cargo hatchways being on each side of the ship. Not
to be confused with the *Minnesota* which was on the London–New York service
up to 1930, this was a British registry vessel, formerly the Red Star Line's *Zee-
land*. She was chartered by the Atlantic Transport Company of West Virginia
during the Great War to run with the chartered *Mongolia* and *Manchuria* of the
Pacific Mail Line, to maintain the A.T.L. service between London and New
York, afterwards bought by them.

1904, April. Launched. The largest vessel to dock in London up to the
year 1924.

1923, Nov. Sold to German firm of shipbreakers.

1924. Broken up at Wilhelmshaven.

MINNESOTA

No. 13. WARWICK CASTLE. 1930

OWNERS:	Union-Castle Mail Steamship Co., Ltd.
SERVICE:	Southampton–Cape.
NAT. & PORT:	British. London.
BUILDERS:	Messrs. Harland & Wolff, Ltd., Belfast, 1930.
TONNAGE:	20,445 tons gross.
DIMENSIONS:	650 ft. lg. b.p. x 75 ft. beam x 44·5 ft. depth. Drt. 32 ft. 1 in. 5 decks.
ENGINES:	2 Harland-B. & W. 8 cyl. D.A. 4 st. Oil Motors, 14,000 b.h.p. Twin screw. Normal speed 16 knots.
EL. LT. & PWR.:	4 six-cyl. Oil Engine-generators.
PAINTWORK:	Union Castle grey hull, red boot-topping, white upper works, funnels red with black top.
COMPLEMENT:	760 1st, 2nd and cabin class passengers.

Sister ship *Winchester Castle*.

De luxe dining saloon, decorated in ivory and rose with wide handsome curtains in old rose damask cleverly arranged with concealed lighting, and a noble picture of Warwick Castle, placed in the centre of the after-end, completes a most agreeable room. The 1st class lounge is a beautiful room, modern but influenced by the Adam style. Swimming pool, gymnasium and Elizabethan smoking room are spacious. Very excellent 2nd class and tourist accommodation is provided.

1933, June. Her Commander, Capt. George Owens, Commodore of Union-Castle fleet, retired.

1936, Jan. Capt. Morton Betts retired from command. In July, 1933, he was appointed Commodore to the Union-Castle fleet.

WARWICK CASTLE

No. 14. CARINTHIA. 1925

OWNERS:	The Cunard White Star Line.
SERVICE:	Liverpool–Boston–New York. Cruising.
NAT. & PORT:	British. Liverpool.
BUILDERS:	Vickers, Ltd., Barrow in Furness, 1925.
TONNAGE:	20,227 tons gross.
DIMENSIONS:	624 ft. long oa. × 73.5 ft. beam × 45 ft. depth. 5 decks.
ENGINES:	4 sets of steam turbines, 12,500 s.h.p. Twin screw. Normal speed 16·5 knots.
BOILERS:	3 D.E. and 3 S.E. boilers, steam pr. 220 lbs. per sq. in., superheated to 300 degrees F.
PAINTWORK:	Hull black with white line above red boot-topping, upper works white, funnel red with 3 black rings and black top. (Hull white on cruising service with green boot-topping.)
COMPLEMENT:	1,650 passengers and 450 officers and crew.

The largest of the five Cunard post-war intermediate size liners, which have been so popular both on the regular service and on cruises.

A notable feature is the excellence and comfort of the 3rd class accommodation. In the 3rd class dining room small tables are provided for parties of friends. There is a smoking room, general room with small library and a shop provided for the 3rd class passengers. The 1st class restaurant is known as the Adam Restaurant and is a very beautiful room, a feature being the silver lamp standards on each table. The sports arena covers 5,000 square feet and extends through two decks. It comprises swimming pool, gymnasium and rackets court, shower baths and electric baths for massage treatment. On "C" deck is found the tourist class smoke room and the tourist lounge with its well stocked library. "A" deck has the beautiful 1st class smoking room which is modelled after the house of El Greco, the great Spanish painter who lived in Toledo in the fifteenth century. This room contains an American bar.

The 1st class lounge is typically English, the furnishing and decorations representing the period of William of Orange. The garden lounges have an improved type of window which gives the effect of a large verandah overlooking the sea. On the boat-deck there are thirty lifeboats and two motor launches and the wide open space is known as the sun deck.

In 1924 the 2nd class accommodation was changed to tourist class.

1932, Dec. Refitted in London for world cruise, left Southampton on December 14th for short West Indies cruise and left New York on January 7th, 1933, on her famous world cruise, of 40,000 miles, visiting more than forty ports, including Tristan de Cunha, the Empire's loneliest island.

1933, Sept. 30th. Received S O S from the Latvian steamer *Andromeda* which later sank after striking a submerged object eighty miles west of Ushant. The steamship *Hartside* saved the crew of the *Andromeda* and the *Carinthia* put back on her course having been too far away to render assistance.

1936, Jan. Transferred to New York–West Indies service.

CARINTHIA

No. 15. KUNGSHOLM. 1928

OWNERS:	Swedish-America Line. A./B. Svenska Amerika Linien.
SERVICE:	Gothenburg–New York.
NAT. & PORT:	Swedish. Gothenburg.
BUILDERS:	Blohm & Voss, Komandit Ges. auf Aktein, Hamburg, Germany, 1928.
TONNAGE:	20,223 tons gross.
DIMENSIONS:	594·5 ft. lg. oa. x 78 ft. beam. 4 decks.
ENGINES:	Two 8 cyl. 4 st D.A. Oil engines. 15,000 s.h.p. By Burmeister & Wain, Copenhagen. Oil fuel bunkers for 2,400 tons. Twin screw. Normal speed 18 knots.
EL. LT. & PWR.:	3 Diesel-engine-generators each 450 k.w. at 220 V.
PAINTWORK:	Hull and upper works white, red boot-topping, funnels buff with a blue disc on each side bearing 3 golden crowns.
COMPLEMENT:	115 1st, 490 2nd, 970 3rd class passengers. Officers and crew 340.

She is indeed a "Home for Kings," she is the largest of the Three White Viking ships of the line, and the largest and fastest ship owned in the Northern Countries. She is a beautiful and popular ship. Her hull is divided into eleven watertight compartments making her practically unsinkable, and she is equipped with twenty-two lifeboats and two larger motor lifeboats, all mounted on Wellin patent davits, her equipment includes a Sperry auto compass, course recorder, rudder angle indicator, etc.

Her lovely public rooms offer a welcome change from the usual period rooms to be found in most liners, being of a quiet, restful dignity in the ultra modern Swedish artistic manner. The decorations were entrusted to Mr. Carl Bergsten, one of Sweden's foremost decorative artists, and everyone who sees the result of his efforts must agree that the company's choice has been amply rewarded. The music room is the most strikingly beautiful room, panelled in sycamore and with a carved ceiling of African pear and alabaster, ebony columns with gold, wood and enamel inlays; connoisseurs say it is one of the most beautiful modern rooms afloat. Forward of the music room are two galleries one on each side of the vessel, each flanked by four columns of macassar ebony. Aft of the music room is the smoke room where instead of the usual oak panelling and furniture there is a wonderful colour scheme in red, gold and black which is very unique and attractive, enhanced by the lattice windows. The entrance hall has a roof cupola in pearl grey and the ceiling has a deep walnut frieze inlaid with silver. The library has walls covered with pigskin and a carved ceiling of walnut. The dining room is a vision of grey and red, the walls being pearl grey and the carpets red. The 2nd and 3rd class are also splendidly accommodated. The large swimming pool is 44 ft. long by 21 ft. wide, with a bar and spectators' balcony alongside.

1928, Nov. 11th. She left Hamburg after her sea trials for Gothenburg where she received a great welcome, thousands of people lining the quays to cheer her advent to her home port; on Nov. 24th, 1928, she left on her maiden voyage to New York.

KUNGSHOLM

No. 16. FRANCONIA. 1923

OWNERS:	Cunard White Star Line, Ltd.
SERVICE:	Atlantic and Cruising.
NAT. & PORT:	British. Liverpool.
BUILDERS:	Messrs. John Brown & Co., Ltd., Clydebank, N.B., 1923.
TONNAGE:	20,175 tons gross.
DIMENSIONS:	601·3 ft. lg. b.p. x 73·7 ft. beam x 40·6 ft. depth. 5 decks.
ENGINES:	2 sets of steam turbines, 12,500 s.h.p. Twin screw. Normal speed 16½ knots.
BUILDERS:	3 D.E. and 3 S.E. boilers, stm. pr. 220 lbs., 200 deg. S.H. Oil fuel.
PAINTWORK:	White hull with green boot-topping, white upper works, funnel red with 3 black rings and black top.
COMPLEMENT:	1,650 passengers and 450 officers and crew.

The second of the five sister cabin liners.

The previous *Franconia* of 1911, a vessel of 18,000 tons, was torpedoed during the war.

1923, June. Launched.

1931, Jan. Chartered by Furness Withy & Co., to take the place of the *Bermuda*, burnt out while refitting at Belfast, on New York–Bermuda run and pending replacement.

1934, Jan. 9th. Left New York at midnight on five months' cruise covering 37,500 miles at a fare of from 305 guineas, with approximately 400 passengers. Was previously redecorated throughout at great expense.

1935, Sept. 26th. It was announced that she would replace the *Homeric* on a cruise commencing Sept. 28th.

FRANCONIA

45

No. 17. DUCHESS OF BEDFORD. 1928

OWNERS: Canadian Pacific S.S., Ltd.

SERVICE: Liverpool–Quebec and Cruising.

NAT. & PORT: British. London.

BUILDERS: Messrs. John Brown & Co., Ltd., Clydebank, N.B., 1928.

TONNAGE: 20,123 tons gross.

DIMENSIONS: 582 ft. lg. b.p. x 75 ft. beam x 41 ft. depth. 4 decks.

ENGINES: 6 steam turbines, sin. red. grd. to 2 screw shafts, 18,000 s.h.p. Twin screw. Normal speed 17½ knots.

BOILERS: 6 water tube, 370 lbs. stm. pr., 700 deg. S.H. F.D. Oil fuel.

PAINTWORK: Black hull with green boot-topping, white upper works, buff funnels.

COMPLEMENT: 600 cabin, 500 tourist, 500 3rd class passengers.

Together with her three sister ships, which are all identical in appearance and design, they have all the latest modern improvements in British shipbuilding and decoration, to make them comfortable and sumptuous. Spacious accommodation is provided and promenade space on three decks. Revolving glass doors lead into the entrance hall, a large observation drawing room, lounge, ballroom in stately Empire style, and dining room in ivory and oak grey with card room, cosy writing room, nursery, gymnasium are provided for the comfort of passengers.

1932, Nov. Made her record passage from Montreal to Greenock in 6 days 1 hour, at an average speed of 18·5 knots.

1933, Nov. 27th. Was held up in St. Lawrence River by snow, ice and fog, together with a score of steamers.

DUCHESS OF BEDFORD

[By courtesy of the Canadian Pacific Line

No. 18. DUCHESS OF ATHOLL. 1928

OWNERS:	Canadian Pacific S.S., Ltd.
SERVICE:	Liverpool–Quebec.
NAT. & PORT:	British. London.
BUILDERS:	Sir Wm. Beardmore & Co., Ltd., Dalmuir, Glasgow, N.B., 1928.
TONNAGE:	20,119 tons gross.
DIMENSIONS:	582 ft. lg. b.p. x 75 ft. beam x 41 ft. depth. 4 decks.
ENGINES:	6 steam turbines, sin. red. grd., 18,000 s.h.p. Twin screw. Normal speed 17½ knots.
BOILERS:	6 water tube, 370 lbs. stm. pr., 700 deg. F. S.H. Oil fuel.
PAINTWORK:	Hull black, boot-topping green, upper works white, funnels buff.
COMPLEMENT:	600 cabin, 500 tourist, 500 3rd class passengers.

Identical in appearance and design to her sister ships *Duchess of Bedford*, *Duchess of York* and *Duchess of Richmond*.

Very luxurious cabin class steamers.

1933, March 29th. Left Liverpool on cruise, visiting Morocco, Italy, French Riviera, Spain and Balearic Islands.

1933, Dec. Brought over Canadian bullion gold worth £1,500,000 for the Mint.

1934, Dec. Capt. A. H. Hall of the *Beaverburn* appointed her Commander.

1935, Oct. She arrived at Liverpool three days late, having lost her rudder; she was steered by her propellers. When off Liverpool tugs attempted to tow her in but owing to a gale and heavy seas the tow ropes snapped and she remained out at sea until the weather eased up, and was then brought in and safely berthed in dock.

DUCHESS OF ATHOLL

OWNERS:	Union-Castle Mail Steamship Co., Ltd.
SERVICE:	Southampton–South Africa.
NAT. & PORT:	British. London.
BUILDERS:	Harland & Wolff, Ltd., Belfast, 1930.
TONNAGE:	20,109 tons gross.
DIMENSIONS:	630·5 ft. lg. b.p. x 75·5 ft. beam x 44·5 ft. depth. 5 decks.
ENGINES:	2 Harland-B. & W. 8 cyl. D.A. 4 st. Oil Engines. Cyls. 33 in. dia 63 in. stroke, 98 r., 14,000 s.h.p. Twin screw. Normal speed 16 kn
COMPLEMENT:	756 1st, 2nd and tourist class passengers.
PAINTWORK:	Union-Castle grey hull, red boot-topping, white upper works, funn red with black tops.

Sister ship *Warwick Castle*.

The 1st class dining saloon is approached from the main staircase through lofty and dignified lobby, designed and coloured in harmony with the salo The saloon is in the style of "William and Mary," with mahogany furnitu The general colour scheme is a pleasant cool green, light in tone, the walls bei relieved with pale amber bowl electric light fittings and old gold curtains. T smoking room is furnished in old oak with an old Dutch angle fireplace, the co tail bar decorations follows the Dutch motif with a low barrel roof, the swi ming pool in blue Delft tiles is very attractive, the lounge is a lofty and handso room with tall mullioned windows and heavy oak beams across the ceiling, the old Colonial style. The library is a quiet, restrained seventeenth centu "Dutch" room; there is also a beautiful verandah café, and a well equipp gymnasium. Second class and tourist accommodation is also on a fine scale.

1936, Feb. 16th. When homeward bound from South Africa she w aground off Portland Bill. (Capt. Kerby in command.)

1936, March. The purser, Mr. Walker Shilling, of London, fell overboa and was drowned.

WINCHESTER CASTLE

[By courtesy of Union-Castle Line

No. 20. CARNARVON CASTLE. 1926

OWNERS:	Union-Castle Mail Steamship Co., Ltd.
SERVICE:	Southampton–East, West and South Africa.
NAT. & PORT:	British. London.
BUILDERS:	Harland & Wolff, Ltd., Belfast, 1926.
TONNAGE:	20,063 tons gross.
DIMENSIONS:	655·75 ft. lg. oa. x 73·5 ft. beam x 45·5 ft. depth. Drt. 32 ft. 8½ in. 5 decks.
ENGINES:	2 Harland-B. & W. D.A. 4 st. 8 cyl. Oil Engines. Cyls. 33 in. dia. x 63 in. stk., 14,000 s.h.p. capable of developing 20,000 I.H.P. Twin screw. Normal speed 16 knots.
PAINTWORK:	Hull Union-Castle grey, boot-topping red, upper works white, funnels red with black tops.
COMPLEMENT:	1st class, 2nd class and tourist, with crew, 1,500 persons.

Very similar in design and appearance to the *Warwick Castle* and *Winchester Castle*.

The first of the Union-Castle big motor ships.

The entrances and staircase are panelled in natural sycamore, natural mahogany is employed for the pilastered door and window casings.   Dining saloon in the English Renaissance period at its best, with windows having boldly enriched architraves.   Lounge is designed in Louis XVI style.   Reading and writing room is in the same style, and has windows on three sides.   Smoking room is a snug retreat in Dutch style of the latter half of the seventeenth century.   A verandah café is based on the lines of a famous Stoep at Pretoria.   The 2nd class and tourist passengers are also well catered for in the usual good style of the Company.

CARNARVON CASTLE

OWNERS:	The Orient Line.
SERVICE:	London–Ceylon–Australia and Cruising.
NAT. & PORT:	British. Barrow.
BUILDERS:	Vickers, Ltd., Barrow, 1925.
TONNAGE:	20,032 tons gross.
DIMENSIONS:	658 ft. lg. oa., 632 ft. lg. b.p. x 75 ft. beam x 33 ft. depth. 5 decks
ENGINES:	6 steam turbines, sin. red. grd., 20,000 s.h.p. Twin screw. Norma speed 20 knots.
BOILERS:	6 D.E. and 4 S.E. boilers, stm. pr. 215 lbs. F.D. Oil fuel.
PAINTWORK:	Hull black, boot-topping red, upper works white, funnels buff with black-painted cowl tops.
COMPLEMENT:	550 1st class, 1,250 3rd class passengers.

Sister ships: *Orontes, Orford, Oronsay* and *Orama*.

The large number of single berth rooms and the exceptionally large open decks make these ships exceedingly popular cruising liners. The Orient Line having commenced cruises in 1889 with the *Chimborazo* and *Caronne*. Dining saloon is a remarkably fine room in cream and grey, lounge with an area of 2,000 square feet with Sienna marble columns and door architraves contrasts agreeably with the cream and gold colour scheme. Smoke room is thoroughly English in character, with panelled walls of unpolished cedar wood, and large bay windows. A distinctly restful writing room, quiet in decoration is also provided, and also a café.

[By courtesy of the Orient Line

OTRANTO

DUCHESS OF RICHMOND. 1928

OWNERS:	The Canadian Pacific S.S., Ltd.
SERVICE:	Liverpool–Quebec.
NAT. & PORT:	British. London.
BUILDERS:	Messrs. John Brown & Co., Ltd., Clydebank, N.B., 1928
TONNAGE:	20,022 tons gross.
DIMENSIONS:	581·5 ft. lg. b.p. x 75 ft. beam x 41 ft. depth. 4 decks.
ENGINES:	6 steam turbines, sin. red. grd., 18,000 s.h.p. Twin screw. Normal speed 17½ knots.
BOILERS:	6 water tube, stm. pr., 370 lbs., 700 deg. S.H.
PAINTWORK:	Hull black, boot-topping green, upper works white, funnels buff.
COMPLEMENT:	600 cabin, 500 tourist, 500 3rd class passengers.

Identical in design and appearance to her sister ships.

All very luxurious cabin class steamers, popular both on Canadian trade and cruising.

1934, April. She carried to Gallipoli 700 Gallipoli veterans with their wives and children and anchored in Kheli Bay. The veterans, who included two Generals, visited the thirty-six British cemeteries scattered over the Gallipoli peninsula. Chosen to take T.R.H. the Duke and Duchess of Kent to the West Indies.

[By courtesy of the Canadian Pacific Line

DUCHESS OF RICHMOND

No. 23. DUCHESS OF YORK. 1929

OWNERS:	The Canadian Pacific S.S. Lines.
SERVICE:	Liverpool and Quebec.
NAT. & PORT:	British. London.
BUILDERS:	Messrs. John Brown & Co., Ltd., Clydebank, N.B., 1929.
TONNAGE:	20,022 tons gross.
DIMENSIONS:	581·5 ft. lg. b.p. x 75 ft. beam x 41 ft. depth. 4 decks.
ENGINES:	6 steam turbines, sin. red. grd., 19,000 s.h.p. Twin screw. Normal speed 17½ knots.
BOILERS:	6 water tube, 370 lbs. stm. pr., 700 deg. S.H. F.D. Oil fuel.
PAINTWORK:	Hull black with green boot-topping, white upper works, funnels buff
COMPLEMENT:	600 cabin, 500 tourist, 500 3rd class passengers.

Design and appearance identical with that of her sister ships. Very luxuriou cabin class steamers, exceedingly popular on both Canadian trade and cruising

1933. When in North Atlantic three huge waves swept over her injuring twenty people, including the ship's doctor, Dr. C. Horton, who, with a broke elbow, bravely continued to work in the ship's hospital. She put into St. John's Newfoundland, where the injured were taken to hospital. Furniture and fitting to the value of nearly £500 were smashed by the waves.

[By courtesy of the Canadian Pacific Line

DUCHESS OF YORK

No. 24. ORONSAY. 1925

OWNERS:	Orient Line, London.
SERVICE:	London–Ceylon–Australia, and Cruising.
NAT. & PORT:	British. Glasgow.
BUILDERS:	Messrs. John Brown & Co., Ltd., Clydebank, N.B., 1925.
TONNAGE:	20,001 tons gross.
DIMENSIONS:	633 ft. lg. x 75 ft. beam x 33 ft. depth. 5 decks.
ENGINES:	6 steam turbines, sin. red. grd., 20,000 s.h.p. Twin screw. Normal speed 20 knots.
BOILERS:	6 D.E. and 4 S.E. boilers, 215 lbs. stm. pr. F.D. Oil fuel.
PAINTWORK:	Black hull, boot-topping red, white upper works, funnels buff with black-painted cowl top.
COMPLEMENT:	550 1st and 1,000 3rd class passengers.

Sister ship to *Otranto*, *Orontes*, *Orford* and *Orama*.   All very similar in appearance and design, a special feature being the very large amount of deck space available for recreation—a very necessary feature on long voyages and cruising.   The dining room is spacious and sumptuous, well lighted and perfectly ventilated; the walls are panelled and painted in tones of ivory in Louis XVI style.   The bronze lighting fittings and distinctive character of the furniture is of special note.   The lounge is remarkable for its fine architectural proportions and its air of luxury.   There are forty-one windows in this room.   The Italian walnut panelled walls of the smoke room are enhanced by beautiful carvings.   An Adam style drawing room is very popular with the ladies who find its colour scheme in ivory and wedgwood blue very restful.   A foyer and a verandah café are also provided.

1931.   Opened the new Lock entrance to Tilbury Docks.

1936, Jan.   Following new regulations made by the Australian Government, she made the first passenger call of the Line at Hobart, Tasmania, carrying 250 inter-colonial passengers.

ORONSAY

No. 25. ORONTES. 1929

OWNERS:	Orient Line, London.
SERVICE:	London–Ceylon–Australia, and Cruising.
NAT. & PORT:	British. Barrow.
BUILDERS:	Vickers, Armstrongs, Ltd., Barrow, 1929.
TONNAGE:	19,970 tons gross.
DIMENSIONS:	664 ft. lg. o.a., 632 ft. lg. b.p. x 75 ft. beam x 33 ft. depth. 5 decks.
ENGINES:	6 steam turbines, sin. red. grd., 20,000 s.h.p. Twin screw. Normal speed 20 knots.
BOILERS:	6 D.E. and 2 S.E. boilers, 215 lbs. stm. pr. F.D. Oil fuel.
PAINTWORK:	Black hull, red boot-topping, white upper works, buff funnels with black-painted cowl tops.
COMPLEMENT:	500 1st and 1,250 3rd class passengers.

One of the five famous Orient 20,000 tonners, notable for their extreme comfort. The *Orontes* is notable for the considerable number of cabins with private bathrooms attached, and all 1st class cabins have a window or a porthole. Has the usual Orient feature of great open deck spaces and an open air swimming bath. The public rooms are of the same high standard as the other ships of the line.

1933, Jan. Did a six weeks' trip to West Indies.

1933, Feb. A ship's boy, late of the Gravesend sea school, distinguished himself; he discovered a fire in a cabin and knowing what a loss of a few minutes may mean in such circumstances he set about the job himself; getting a chemical extinguisher he put out the outbreak and then went and reported the occurrence to the Chief Steward. He was complimented by the Captain.

1934, April. Stranded on Gallipoli coast during a cruise, but soon refloated undamaged.

1935, Jan. 3rd. Inward bound from Australia she was held up in the Thames estuary with other vessels by a dense fog.

ORONTES

[By courtesy of the Orient Line

No. 26. ORFORD. 1928

OWNERS: Orient Line, London.
SERVICE: London–Ceylon–Australia, and Cruising.
NAT. & PORT: British. Barrow.
BUILDERS: Vickers, Ltd., Barrow, 1928.
TONNAGE: 19,941 tons gross.
DIMENSIONS: 650 ft. lg. o.a., 632 ft. b.p. x 75 ft. beam x 33 ft. depth. 5 decks.
ENGINES: 6 steam turbines, sin. red. grd., 20,000 s.h.p. Twin screw. Normal speed 20 knots.
BOILERS: 6 D.E. and 2 S.E. boilers, 215 lbs. stm. pr. F.D. Oil fuel.
PAINTWORK: Black hull, red boot-topping, white upper works, buff funnels with black-painted cowl tops.
COMPLEMENT: 520 1st and 1,000 3rd class passengers.

Like her four sister ships she was especially designed for the mail and passenger service between England and Australia, and generally she is exactly similar in design and appearance, having an open air tiled swimming pool and the usual Orient Line's great area of unobstructed deck space.

1932, Dec. Made a cruise to the West Indies.

1934, Dec. 20th. Arrived from Australia having encountered in the Bay of Biscay the full force of a 80-mile-an-hour gale; as she was entering the Channel a huge wave broke over her flooding the lower decks. One of the crew slipped overboard with the out-rushing water, the ship was put about and a lifeboat lowered but he had unfortunately disappeared.

1935, Jan. Her 3rd class accommodation was refitted by the builders and converted into tourist class.

ORFORD

[By courtesy of the Orient Line

No. 27. RELIANCE. 1920
(Ex. Limburgia, Ex. Johann Heinrich Burchard

OWNERS:	Hamburg-Amerika Line.
SERVICE:	Hamburg–New York.
NAT. & PORT:	German. Hamburg.
BUILDERS:	J. C. Teckleburg, Akt. Ges., Wesermonde, Germany, 1920.
TONNAGE:	19,821 tons gross.
DIMENSIONS:	500 ft. lg., 80 ft. beam x 40 ft. depth. 5 decks.
ENGINES:	2 Quad. exp. 4 cyl. recip. engines on outer shafts and 1 low pressure turbine on centre shaft. 16,000 s.h.p. Triple screw. Normal speed 17 knots.
PAINTWORK:	Hull white, red boot-topping, white upper works, buff funnels, with red, white and black tops.
COMPLEMENT:	531 passengers and 393 Officers and crew.

Sister ship to *Resolute*.

1914. Laid down for the Hamburg–Amerika Line but construction was held up during the war.

1920. Completed and given by German Government to Holland as reparation for her losses due to submarines during war. The Allies protested and she was transferred to the United States.

Sold to the United States Line and run under Panama flag.

Sold with her sister ship to Hamburg–Amerika Line and was the Line's first post-war transatlantic liner.

RELIANCE

[By courtesy of the Hamburg-Amerika Line

No. 28. CARONIA. 1905

OWNERS: Cunard Line.
SERVICE: Liverpool–Boston and New York.
NAT. & PORT: British. Liverpool.
BUILDERS: Messrs. J. Brown & Co., Ltd., Clydebank, N.B., 1905.
TONNAGE: 19,782 tons gross.
DIMENSIONS: 650 ft. lg. x 72 ft. beam x 44 ft. depth. 4 decks.
ENGINES: 2 Quad. exp. 4 cyl. recip. steam engines, 18,000 s.h.p. Twin scre
Normal speed 18 knots.
BOILERS: 5 D.E. and 5 S.E. boilers, 210 lbs. stm. pr. F.D. Oil fuel.
PAINTWORK: Hull black, red boot-topping with white dividing line, upper wo
white, funnels red with 3 black rings and black top.
COMPLEMENT: 425 cabin class, 365 tourist class, 650 3rd class passengers.

With her sister ship *Carmania* they commenced a new era in the intermedi
speed cabin class liner, very popular for their steadiness in all weathers.

1914–18. Did much war service very successfully.

1920. Refitted and converted to oil burning.

1926. Transferred to London–New York service.

1932, Jan. Sold for scrapping to Messrs. Hughes Bolchow Shipbreak
Company, for about £20,000 with delivery in July.

1932, Nov. Was resold to Japanese shipbreakers for £25,000 plus £14,0
for delivery to Japan. Sailed to Japan under the name of *Taiseiyo Maru*.

CARONIA

No. 29. ORAMA. 1924

OWNERS:	Orient Line, London.
SERVICE:	London–Ceylon–Australia, and Cruising.
NAT. & PORT:	British. Barrow.
BUILDERS:	Messrs. Vickers, Ltd., Barrow, 1924.
TONNAGE:	19,777 tons gross.
DIMENSIONS:	658 ft. lg. o.a., 632 ft. lg. b.p. x 75 ft. beam x 33 ft. depth. 5 d
ENGINES:	2 sets of 6 steam turbines, sin. red. grd., 20,000 s.h.p. Twin sc Normal speed 20 knots.
BOILERS:	6 D.E. and 4 S.E. boilers, 215 lbs. stm. pr. F.D. Oil fuel.
PAINTWORK:	Hull black, red boot-topping, upperworks white, buff funnels black-painted cowl tops. Was at one time experimentally painte the same colours as the *Orion:* Hull corn coloured, green boot-top upper works white, funnels buff with black-painted cowl tops.
COMPLEMENT:	550 1st class, 1,000 3rd class passengers.

The first of the Orient five 20,000 tonners, which made such a big step forw in the Australian trade. Like her sister ships she has a large number of si berth rooms and great open deck spaces, features which made these vesse popular for cruising. Saloon dining room is a spacious finely proportic room; the colour scheme suggests mellow old ivory with mahogany furnit The lounge is in a delightful grey, is 100 ft. long and has seating accommoda for over 250. The café is a thoroughly English room in the seventeenth cen style, with seating accommodation for 100. The writing and smoking rc are also on the same luxurious scale.

1933. A luncheon was held on board at Tilbury to mark the commencen of the new Australian butter scheme.

1935. Third class accommodation was converted into tourist.

1936, April. When on voyage from Barrow to London after refit and c haul, without passengers or cargo, was in collision with *Sveti Duje* (3,624 gross), bound from Rotterdam for Servola with a cargo of coal. Both ve received some damage and docked at Tilbury for repairs.

ORAMA

No. 30. SCYTHIA. 1920

OWNERS:	Cunard White Star Line.
SERVICE:	Liverpool–Boston–New York, and Cruising.
NAT. & PORT:	British. Liverpool.
BUILDERS:	Vickers, Ltd., Barrow, 1920.
TONNAGE:	19,761 tons gross.
DIMENSIONS:	600·7 ft. lg. x 73 ft. beam x 40 ft. depth. Drt. 31 ft. 8 in. 4 decks.
ENGINES:	2 sets of 6 steam turbines, dou. red. grd., 12,500 s.h.p. Twin screw. Normal speed 16½ knots.
BOILERS:	3 D.E. and 3 S.E. boilers, 220 lbs. stm. pr. Oil fuel.
PAINTWORK:	Black hull, red boot-topping with white dividing line, white upper works, red funnels with 3 black rings and black top.
COMPLEMENT:	2,000 passengers in cabin, tourist and 3rd class.

One of the Cunard post-war cabin class liners which have proved themselves so popular both on the Atlantic and cruising. They played an important part in the tremendous Eastbound travel which occurred in the 1920's.

First passenger liner to be built by Messrs. Vickers.

Skilfully designed for service in any climate with an up-to-date system of ventilation, the *Scythia* combines all the qualities of a perfect Atlantic liner. The accommodation is excellent and beautiful.

1921, Aug. 20th. Maiden voyage. From Liverpool to New York.

1924. Tourist class accommodation was inaugurated.

SCYTHIA

[By courtesy of Cunard White Star Line

No. 31. LOMBARDIA. 1914

(Ex. Resolute, Ex. Brabantia, Ex. William O'Swald)

OWNERS: Italia Lines.

SERVICE: Hamburg–New York. When in Hamburg–Amerika Line.

NAT. & PORT: German. Hamburg.

BUILDERS: J. C. Teckleburg, Akt. Ges., Wesermunde, Germany, 1914.

TONNAGE: 19,703 tons gross.

DIMENSIONS: 500 ft. lg. x 80 ft. beam x 40 ft. depth. 5 decks.

ENGINES: 2 Quad. exp. 4 cyl. recip. engines on outer shafts, one low pressu
turbine on centre shaft. 16,000 s.h.p. Triple screw. Normal spe
17 knots.

PAINTWORK: Hull white, red boot-topping, white upper works, buff funnels wi
red, white and black tops.

COMPLEMENT: 520 passengers, 393 officers and crew (under Hamburg-Ameri
management).

Sister ship to *Reliance*.

1914. Laid down for Hamburg–Amerika Line but construction held up duri
the war.

1920. Completed and given by German Government to Holland as repar
tion for her losses due to submarines during the war. The Allies protested a
she was handed over to the United States.

Sold to the United States Line and run under Panama Flag.

Sold to Hamburg–Amerika Line with her sister ship. They were the Line
first big post war transatlantic ships.

1935, Aug. 22nd. It was announced that she had been sold to the Itali
Government to be used as a troopship. Price said to be £80,000. Re-nam
Lombardia.

1936. Taken over by "Italia" Lines.

LOMBARDIA Ex. RESOLUTE

No. 32. LACONIA. 1922

As Scythia

OWNERS:	Cunard White Star Line.
SERVICE:	Liverpool–Boston–New York, and Cruising.
NAT. & PORT:	British. Liverpool.
BUILDERS:	Swan, Hunter & Wigham Richardson, Ltd., Newcastle-on-Tyne 1922.
TONNAGE:	19,695 tons gross.
DIMENSIONS:	610 ft. lg. x 73½ ft. beam x 31·9 ft. depth. Drt. 31 ft. 8 in. 4 decks.
ENGINES:	2 sets of 6 steam turbines, dou. red. grd. 12,500 s.h.p. By Wallsend S. & Eng. Co., Ltd., Newcastle. Twin screw. Normal speed 16½ knots
BOILERS:	3 D.E. & 3 S.E. boilers, 220 lbs. stm. pr. F.D. Oil fuel.
PAINTWORK:	Hull black, red boot-topping with white dividing line, upper works white, funnel red with three black rings and black top.
COMPLEMENT:	2,000 passengers in cabin, tourist and 3rd classes when on Atlantic service.

Previous ship of same name a vessel of 18,000 tons built in 1913, was sunk during war. Fourth of the five Cunard post war cabin liners. Fitted with anti-rolling tanks (Frahms). The first British liner to be so equipped.

1924. Tourist class inaugurated.

1933. Brought a record cargo of fruit from New York and Boston to Liverpool numbering 41,000 cases of grape fruit, apples and plums.

1934, Sept. 24th. On voyage from Liverpool to New York was in collision at 2.50 a.m. off Cape Cod with the U.S. freighter *Pan Royal* of Wilmington, Del. After standing by for half an hour to see extent of damage both vessels proceeded on their way, damage very slight.

LACONIA

[By courtesy of Cunard White Star Line

No. 33. VICEROY OF INDIA. 1929

OWNERS:	The Peninsular & Oriental Steam Navigation Co.
SERVICE:	London–Bombay, and Cruising.
NAT. & PORT:	British. Glasgow.
BUILDERS:	Messrs. A. Stephens & Sons, Ltd., Glasgow, 1929.
TONNAGE:	19,648 tons gross.
DIMENSIONS:	586·1 ft. lg. x 76·2 ft. beam x 41·5 ft. depth. 5 decks.
ENGINES:	2 steam turbo-generators, each 9,000 k.w., 2,690/3,110 r.p.m. 3 phase 2,720 volts. 2 electric shaft motors on screw shafts, each 8,500 s.h.p 109 r.p.m. 3 phase, 3,150 volts. At reduced powers of 11,600 s.h.p and under only one turbo-generator is required for supplying pow to both motors, thus maximum economy in fuel is obtained. Variatic of propeller speed in either direction is obtained by varying the turbin speed. 19,000 s.h.p. By B.T.H. Co., Ltd., Rugby. Twin screw Normal speed 19 knots.
BOILERS:	6 water tube, 400 lb. stm. pr. Stm. pr. 700 deg. super heat, F.l Oil fuel.
PAINTWORK:	Hull black, with white band, red boot-topping, upper works ston funnels black.
COMPLEMENT:	683 passengers.

First big British turbo-electric liner and the most luxurious liner to India

Made new record for London–Bombay service, average speed between por being 17·92 knots. Voyage in 16 days 1 hr. 42 mins.

Has made a record number of voyages and cruises, spending very little tin in port; seldom has a vessel been worked so hard and her machinery has stood th strain without trouble.

Her Chief and Third Officers received medals from the Greek Governmer for the rescue of the crew of the *Theodoros Bulgaris*.

1934, Feb. 12th. Was struck by unknown ship in fog while at anchor an sustained a little damage above waterline.

1935, Sept. 5th. Answered S O S sent out by the *Doric* which had bee damaged in collision with the French steamer *Formigny* off the coast of Portug; in a dense fog. Within three hours of the crash all the *Doric's* passengers had bee transferred to the *Viceroy of India* and the *Orion*.

1935, Sept. 7th. Arrived at Tilbury with the *Doric's* passengers.

It was only on the day previous when she was at Lisbon, September 5t 1935, that her commander, Capt. Thorton, received intimation that he had bee appointed Commodore of the P. & O. fleet.

1936, April. Capt. E. J. Thornton, Commander and Commodore of th P. & O. fleet, retired from his command and from the service of the Line. Cap E. A. J. W. Carter, R.N.R., was appointed to the command of the *Viceroy* *India*.

VICEROY OF INDIA

No. 34. SAMARIA. 1921

As Scythia

OWNERS:	Cunard White Star Line.
SERVICE:	Liverpool–Boston–New York, and Cruising.
NAT. & PORT:	British. Liverpool.
BUILDERS:	Messrs. Cammell Laird & Co., Ltd., Birkenhead, 1921.
TONNAGE:	19,597 tons gross.
DIMENSIONS:	623·75 ft. lg. o.a., 601·5 ft. lg. b.p. x 73·7 ft. beam x 40 ft depth. 5 decks.
ENGINES:	2 sets of six turbines, dou. red. grd., 12,500 s.h.p. Twin screw. Normal speed 16½ knots.
BOILERS:	3 D.E. and 3 S.E. boilers, 220 lbs. stm. pr. F.D. Oil fuel.
PAINTWORK:	Black hull, red boot-topping with white dividing line, white upper works, funnel red with three black rings and black top.
COMPLEMENT:	2,000 passengers in three classes on Atlantic service, 600 in one class when cruising.

Fifth of the five Cunard post-war cabin liners. She enjoys the same popularity as her sister ships both on Atlantic and cruising.

Has very splendid accommodation and her cabin smoke room is a wonderful representation of an oak room in an old English inn, possessing an inglenook running one-third of the length. The cabin dining room extends right across the ship and is 64 ft. long; surmounting the room is an open wrought iron balustrade behind which the orchestra is placed.

1924. Tourist class inaugurated.

1934. Commenced ten cruises from London (Tilbury).

SAMARIA

No. 35. CARMANIA. 1905

OWNERS:	Cunard Line.
SERVICE:	Liverpool–Boston–New York.
NAT. & PORT:	British. Liverpool.
BUILDERS:	Messrs. John Brown & Co., Ltd., Clydebank, N.B., 1905.
TONNAGE:	19,524 tons gross.
DIMENSIONS:	650 ft. lg. x 72 ft. beam x 40 ft. depth. 4 decks.
ENGINES:	3 steam turbines. 18,000 s.h.p. Triple screw. Normal speed 18 knots.
BOILERS:	8 D.E. and 5 S.E. boilers, stm. pr. 195 lbs. F.D.
PAINTWORK:	Hull black, boot-topping red with white dividing line, upper works white, funnels red with three black rings and black top.
COMPLEMENT:	425 cabin, 365 tourist, 650 3rd class.

The first turbine Cunarder and with the *Victorian* first Atlantic turbine liners. With her sister ship *Caronia* the Cunard Company made the experiment of building two ships exactly alike except for engines, to test the results of turbine against quadruple expansion engines, before deciding on the engines for the projected two express liners (*Lusitania* and *Mauretania*), and the results obtained proved the greater efficiency of the turbine as well as greater reserve power, the *Carmania* always proving the faster of the two as well as the most economical.

1913. Oct. With Capt. Barr in command went to the rescue of the Italian emigrant ship *Volturno* on fire in Atlantic. Capt. Barr and officers received medals for their work.

1914, August. On her arrival at Liverpool was speedily got ready for war service as an armed auxiliary cruiser and was commissioned by the Admiralty and immediately sent out to search for enemy raiders; on Sept. 14th she met the German armed merchant cruiser *Cap Trafalgar* and engaged her in action; after a very hot action, the *Cap Trafalgar* sank within two hours of the first gun being fired. The Admiralty complimented the officers and crew in a letter to the owners stating that although she was damaged by no less than seventy-nine shell hits they carried on the fight and brought her safely through. This was the first fight between two modern armed merchant liners.

1914, Sept. Capt. Noel Grant commander.

1921. Refitted and converted to oil fuel and tourist class accommodation provided.

1926. Transferred to London–New York service.

1932, Nov. Sold with her sister ship to ship breakers.

CARMANIA

No. 36. MOUNT VERNON. 1907

(Ex. Kronprinzessin Cecilie)

OWNERS:	United States Navy Department.
SERVICE:	Troopship.
NAT. & PORT:	United States. New York.
BUILDERS:	Vulkan Werkes, Stettin, 1907.
TONNAGE:	19,503 tons gross.
DIMENSIONS:	685 ft. b.p., 72·2 ft. beam, 40·5 ft. depth. 5 decks.
ENGINES:	4 quadruple expansion, 4 cyl. engines, 2 connected to each shaft Total 45,000 I.H.P. Twin screw. Normal speed 23½ knots.
BOILERS:	12 D.E. and 3 S.E. boilers. 225 lbs. per square inch steam pressure.
COMPLEMENT:	

A fine, pre-war, big passenger carrying liner, built especially for emigrant trade. Her accommodation was in keeping with the high standard of the North German Lloyd Company. Between 1907 and 1914 she carried a great many emigrants to the West from Europe. Her record passages were, westward from Cherbourg to Sandy Hook in 5 days 11 hours 9 mins. Average speed of 23·22 knots. Best day's run 590 miles. Eastward, Sandy Hook to Cherbourg 5 days 7 hours 23 mins. Average speed 23·4 knots. Best day's run 560 miles.

1914, Aug. She was at sea on voyage from New York to Bremerhaven when war was declared, with £2,000,000 worth of gold on board. The German authorities, taking no risks of her capture by the Allies, ordered her to return to an American port. She eluded the Allies' naval forces and anchored inside Bar Harbour, Maine. The port not being suitable for a vessel of her size, she was moved to Boston, the Allies giving her a safe conduct, by agreement.

1917. She was taken over by the United States Government and commissioned as a troopship.

1918, Sept. 5th. She was torpedoed off Brest, thirty-six being killed by the explosion. The captain managed to make port, and she arrived in Brest disabled and only just afloat.

She is now a troopship in the United States Navy.

MOUNT VERNON

[By courtesy of Norddeutscher Lloyd Line

No. 37. NEPTUNIA. 1932

OWNERS:	Italia Line. (Cosulich Soc. Triestina di Nav.).
SERVICE:	Trieste–South American ports.
NAT. & PORT:	Italian. Trieste.
BUILDERS:	Cantieri Riuniti Dell Adriatico, Monfalcone, Italy, 1932.
TONNAGE:	19,475 tons gross.
DIMENSIONS:	562·4 ft. lg. o.a., 589·7 ft. lg. b.p. x 76·7 ft. beam x 45·5 ft. depth Drt. 27 ft. 4 decks.
ENGINES:	4 Sulzer type Diesel engines, 2 8 cyls., 2 9 cyls. 123/126 r.p.m. Tot 19,000 s.h.p. Quad screw. Normal speed 19 knots.
EL. LT. & PWR.:	4 Diesel-generators, totalling 2,640 k.w., 230 volts.
PAINTWORK:	Hull black, boot-topping red, upper works white, funnel white wi thin green band and red and black top.
COMPLEMENT:	Cabin class, 175, 3rd. class 709.

Sister ship *Oceania*.

The cabin accommodation is very luxurious and the public rooms large an modern in decoration.

The 3rd class accommodation is very exceptional, having wardrobe and two wash basins with hot water in each cabin.

Trials. A maximum of 21·8 kts. obtained.

1932, Oct. 5th. Left Naples on her maiden voyage to Venice, where reception was held. Leaving on Oct. 6th she arrived at Naples on Oct. 7th doing on the voyage an average speed of twenty knots, and left on her first voyag to Buenos Aires arriving on Oct. 24th.

1935, Feb. Was prepared for transfer to Far Eastern trade. Genoa t Shanghai, calling at Bombay, etc.

NEPTUNIA

No. 38. OCEANIA. 1932

OWNERS:	Italia Line (Cosulich Soc. Triestina di Nav.).
SERVICE:	Trieste–South American ports.
NAT. & PORT:	Italian. Trieste.
BUILDERS:	Cantieri Riuniti Dell Adriatico, Malfalcone, Italy, 1932.
TONNAGE:	19,470 tons gross.
DIMENSIONS:	589·7 ft. lg. o.a., 562 ft. lg. b.p. x 76 ft. beam x 45 ft. depth. Drt 27 ft. 6 in. 4 decks.
ENGINES:	4 "Fiat" 8 cyl. air injection 2 st. d.a. Oil Engines. 120 r.p.m. 22,000 s.h.p. Quad. screw. Normal speed 19 knots.
PAINTWORK:	Hull black, boot-topping red, upper works white, funnel white with thin green band and red and black top.
COMPLEMENT:	200 cabin, 400 3rd, and 650 emigrants. Officers and crew 250.
ON TRIALS:	Did a maximum speed of 23 knots on measured mile. On 9 hour trial did an average speed of 22·12 knots. Largest motor vessel completed in 1933 in the world.

Sister ship to *Neptunia* but with greater engine power and some improvements in accommodation. Very handsome public rooms, with swimming pool, are provided while the 3rd class accommodation is very exceptional. .

1933, April 6th. Maiden voyage from Trieste to Buenos Aires.

1935, Feb. It was announced that she was being refitted for transfer to the Far Eastern trade, Genoa to Shanghai, calling at Bombay, etc.

OCEANIA

No. 39. MONTICELLI. 1902

(Ex. Agamemnon, Ex. Kaiser Wilhelm II)

OWNERS: United States Shipping Board.
SERVICE: New York–Europe.
NAT. & PORT: United States. New York.
BUILDERS: Akt. Ges. Vulcan, Stettin, Germany, 1902.
TONNAGE: 19,361 tons gross.
DIMENSIONS: 684·3 ft. lg. o.a. x 72·3 ft. beam x 40 ft. depth. 5 decks.
ENGINES: 4 Quad. exp. 4 cyl. recip. engines, 2 on ea. screw shaft (a very unusual arrangement). 40,000 s.h.p. Twin screw. Normal speed 23 knots.

Possibly the highest powered ship with reciprocating engines ever built for merchant service.

1902, Aug. 12th. Launched for North German Lloyd Co., as *Kaiser Wilhelm* II.

1903. Maiden voyage, won Atlantic Blue Riband at average speed of 23·57 knots, beating the record of the *Kronprinz Wilhelm* of the same line. This record stood until beaten by the *Lusitania* in 1907.

1913. Was in collision.

1914. Interned in New York.

1917. Taken over by United States War Department and renamed *Agamemnon*, converted into troopship.

1921. Taken over by United States Shipping Board and renamed *Monticelli*.

1933. Sold for scrapping.

MONTICELLI

[By courtesy of Norddeutscher Lloyd Line

89

No. 40. MARNIX VAN ST. ALDEGONDE.
1930

OWNERS:	Nederland N.V. Stoomvaart Maatschappij (The Nederland Line).
SERVICE:	Holland–Dutch East Indies.
NAT. & PORT:	Dutch. Amsterdam.
BUILDERS:	Netherland Shipbuilding Company, Amsterdam, 1930.
TONNAGE:	19,129 tons gross.
DIMENSIONS:	580 ft. lg. x 74 ft. beam x 47·3 ft. depth. 6 decks.
ENGINES:	2 Sulzer-de Schelde Diesel heavy oil engines. 2 cycle, 10 cyl.-engines, totalling 14,000 b.h.p. at 100 r.p.m. by Koninklijke Maatschappij "De Schelde," Flushing. Twin screw. Normal speed 17 knots.
EL. LT. & PWR.:	3 Werkspoor Diesel engine generators, and 1 Sulzer Diesel engine generator with a total output of 1,750 k.w. at 220 volts. There are 4,500 h.p. of electric motors on board, 5,500 lights, 800 fans and 500 k.w. of electric heating apparatus. A powerful stand-by battery is provided to supply power for steering and emergency lighting, in case of failure of power plant. There is also an emergency motor generator fitted on top deck to supply current for radio and emergency lighting.
PAINTWORK:	Hull black, boot-topping red, upper works white, funnels buff with black tops.
COMPLEMENT:	247 1st class, 335 2nd class, 99 3rd class and 46 4th class passengers. 375 officers and crew.

The second of the two big motor ships of the line and the flagship of the fleet. With her sister the *Johan van Oldenbarnevelt*, they are the largest Dutch motor ships.

She was named after the famous Philips Van Marnix, Sire of St. Aldegonde, 1533–1598, whose talents were shown more in his ability as a poet, orator and statesman than as a warrior. He was the right hand man of William of Orange, he was one of the wittiest and most learned men of his time. He is reputed to have written the Dutch national anthem—"Wilhelmus van Nassouwe."

The ship is a roomy and comfortable liner; with her straight stem, cruiser stern, two squat funnels and two masts she makes a picture of modern design. Her public rooms are tastefully decorated and fitted with every comfort, the artistic decorations being by that celebrated artist, Mr. C. A. Leon Cachet. There are 165 1st class cabins, 139 2nd class cabins, 33 3rd class and 8 4th class cabins. Fourteen large and two smaller lifeboats are carried in McLachlin patent davits, providing sufficient emergency accommodation for the whole of the complement of 1,134 persons. A big feature is the large open verandah sports deck behind the funnels, all 1st class cabins are fitted with bedsteads instead of berths. The swimming bath is of neat but rather severe design.

1936, Oct. 8th. She had a fire in No. 2 hold and put in to Ajaccio, Corsica, with the hold flooded. The fire was extinguished and she proceeded on her voyage from Amsterdam for Sourabaya.

[By courtesy of Nederland S.S. Co.

MARNIX VAN ST. ALDEGONDE

OWNERS:	Furness, Withy & Co., Ltd., London. (Bermuda & West Indies S.S. Co., Ltd.)
SERVICE:	New York–Bermuda.
NAT. & PORT:	British. Hamilton, Bermuda.
BUILDERS:	Workman, Clarke & Co., Ltd., Belfast, 1927.
TONNAGE:	19,086 tons gross.
DIMENSIONS:	525·4 ft. lg. b.p. x 74·1 ft. beam x 39·6 ft. depth. 5 decks.
ENGINES:	Four 4 cyl. 2 st. C.S.A. Diesel, heavy oil engines, by Doxford & Sons, Ltd., Sunderland, totalling 18,000 b.m.p.; 2 steam boilers for heating and auxiliaries, 120 lbs. square inch pressure. Quad. screw. 18 knots.
PAINTWORK:	Hull grey, boot-topping green with white dividing line, upper works white, funnels black with two red bands of unequal thickness.

The first of the big luxury liners built for the New York–Bermuda run, she was an ill-fated vessel, although quite successful and popular during the short time she was on service. She was the largest motor vessel built in the British Isles down to date. Early in 1931 she had the misfortune to have her luxurious passenger accommodation burnt out while in port at Hamilton, Bermuda, after the passengers had disembarked. The hull of the ship was undamaged, and she was taken to Belfast, her builders receiving the contract to refit her. Her main engines were not particularly damaged, but the auxiliaries were removed for extensive overhaul in the shops, as they had suffered severely from water damage. The work was well in hand, when, in November, 1931, she again caught alight, and was burned out completely at her berth in the builders' yard. After the fire had been subdued, she was found to be too far gone to be re-fitted and the hull was sold for scrap. While she was being towed away for breaking up she broke from her tugs, and ran ashore, becoming a total loss.

The turbo-electric liner *Queen of Bermuda* was built to replace her, a Cunard liner being chartered to take her place until the arrival of the new ship.

[*By courtesy of Furness Withy & Co., Ltd.*

BERMUDA

No. 42. JOHAN VAN OLDENBARNEVELT.

As Marnix Van St. Aldegonde

OWNERS:	Nederland N.V. Stoomvaart Maatschappij (The Nederland Line).
SERVICE:	Holland–Dutch East Indies.
NAT. & PORT:	Dutch. Amsterdam.
BUILDERS:	Netherland Shipbuilding Co., Ltd., Amsterdam.
TONNAGE:	19,040 tons gross.
DIMENSIONS:	586 ft. lg. o.a. x 74·4 ft. beam x 47·3 ft. depth. 5 decks.
ENGINES:	2 Sulzer de Schelde, 10 cyl. 2 cycle, heavy oil engines totalling 14,000 b.h.p. at 100 r.p.m. Twin screw. 17 knots.
LT. & PWR.	4 auxiliary Diesel generator sets with an output totalling 1,750 k.w.
PAINTWORK:	Hull black, boot-topping red, upper works white, funnels buff with black tops.
COMPLEMENT:	620 1st and 2nd class, 64 3rd class, 50 4th class passengers. 375 officers and crew.

The first of the two big motorships of the line, and with her sister ship the *Marnix Van Sint Aldegonde* they are the largest Dutch motor vessels. Generally similar to her sister ship, her tasteful decorations were by the same artist, Mr. C. A. Leon Cachet. On her trials she made 19 knots. A fine pair of ships that brought a new era in comfort and speed to the route they serve.

[*By courtesy of the Nederland S.S. Line*

JOHAN VAN OLDENBARNEVELT

No. 43. ARUNDEL CASTLE. 1921

OWNERS:	The Union Castle Mail S.S. Company, Ltd., London.
SERVICE:	Southampton–Cape Town via Madeira and Canary Islands.
NAT. & PORT:	British. London.
BUILDERS:	Harland & Wolff, Ltd., Belfast, 1921.
TONNAGE:	19,029 tons gross.
DIMENSIONS:	630·5 ft. lg. o.a. x 72·5 ft. beam x 41·5 ft. depth. 32 ft. 9½ in. drt. 5 decks.
ENGINES:	4 steam turbines geared to the 2 screw shafts. Twin screw. Normal speed 18 knots.
PAINTWORK:	Hull Union-Castle grey, boot-topping red, upper works white, funnels red with black tops.
COMPLEMENT:	234 1st, 300 2nd, and 274 3rd class passengers.

Sister ship *Windsor Castle*. The first of the line's post-war vessels, and the largest to date for the line and on the route.

This splendid pair of four funnelled luxury liners have been very popular on the South African route.

The public rooms are very handsome and are large, well appointed saloons. The sitting room on the port side of the vessel is panelled in oak of a simple character, in the Louis XVI period, and is furnished with easy chairs and small chairs upholstered in a beautiful blue material, with silk curtains of the same colour, making an impressive yet restful room for perfect leisure.

The 1st class dining room with accommodation for 254 passengers is panelled in Georgian fashion, with a note of richness in the floral wreaths which decorate the ceiling, the mahogany furniture is of an early Chippendale character. The reception room adjoining the dining saloon is decorated with the same good taste; here an organ and piano are installed for Church Services on Sundays and concerts during the week. The 1st class smoke room situated on the promenade deck is a long, oak panelled room of the seventeenth century style, lattice windows with flat arched tops add to the effect of a room in a Tudor mansion.

The 1st class lounge forward of the smoking room is a very pleasant bow-windowed room with white panelling of the Louis XVI period, delicately touched here and there with gold. This is essentially the ladies' domain, the drawing room of the ship. There is also provided a restful reading and writing room, situated on the boat deck; this lovely room is panelled in natural colour sycamore wood; bookcases with some 800 volumes provide reading matter for the traveller.

1936, Sept. With the commissioning of the *Athlone Castle*, she was withdrawn from service for re-engining in accordance with the new mail contract of the Line and to bring her into line with the speed of the new ships.

ARUNDEL CASTLE

[By courtesy of the Union-Castle Line

No. 44. WINDSOR CASTLE. 1922

OWNERS:	The Union Castle Mail S.S. Company, Ltd., London.
SERVICE:	Southampton–Capetown via Madeira and Canary Islands.
NAT. & PORT:	British. London.
BUILDERS:	John Brown & Co., Ltd., Clydebank, 1922.
TONNAGE:	18,993 tons gross.
DIMENSIONS:	632·7 ft. lg. o.a. x 72·5 ft. beam x 41·6 ft. depth. 5 decks.
ENGINES:	4 steam turbines, single reduction geared to the 2 screw shafts. Twin screw. Normal speed 18 knots.
PAINTWORK:	Hull Union-Castle grey, boot-topping red, upper works white, funnels red with black tops.
COMPLEMENT:	234 1st, 300 2nd, and 274 3rd class passengers.

Sister ship *Arundel Castle*, the second of the Line's post war ships.

These two fine ships are the last of the Line's tall funnelled vessels, the later ships all having the low squat funnels of the modern motor ship. The *Windsor Castle* and her sister have very beautiful lines and still have a large following of regular travellers.

The accommodation for all three classes is commodious and tasteful, every comfort is provided. Private suites-de-luxe have been arranged on the upper deck consisting of a sitting room, bedroom, bathroom and maids' room. All the 1st class rooms are provided with bedsteads, wardrobes, chest of drawers, folding wash stands, large mirrors, and reading lights over each bed. The 2nd and 3rd classes are also very well catered for. The 2nd class dining room is a particularly cheerful well lighted room, with white walls and a dado of polished mahogany; it has seats for 232 diners. Both ships have straight stems and cruiser sterns as will be seen by the illustrations.

WINDSOR CASTLE

[By courtesy of the Union-Castle Line

No. 45. ALBERTIC. 1921

(Ex. Ohio, Ex. Munchen)

OWNERS:	White Star Line.
SERVICE:	Liverpool–Boston–Montreal and New York.
NAT. & PORT:	British. Liverpool.
BUILDERS:	Akt. Gest, "Weser," Bremen, 1921.
TONNAGE:	18,940 tons gross.
DIMENSIONS:	587 ft. long b.p. x 71.5 ft. beam x 46 ft. depth. 5 decks.
ENGINES:	2 quadruple expansion 4 cyl. engines. 16,000 s.h.p. Twin scr Normal speed 16 knots.
BOILERS:	6 D.E. boilers, 220 lbs. stm. pr. F.D.
PAINTWORK:	Hull black with gold band, boot-topping red, upper works wh funnels buff with black tops.
COMPLEMENT:	580 cabin and 1,700 third class passengers.

Laid down at Bremen for the North German Lloyd Company, and launch as the *Munchen*. Designed for big passenger accommodation at moderate spe Construction was held up during the war.

In 1931 she was ceded to Great Britain by the Treaty of Versailles. Af completion in Germany in 1920, the British Shipping Controller sold her the Royal Mail Steam Packet Company, who renamed her *Ohio* and plac her on the Line's new service from England to New York. When the Roy Mail Steam Packet Company acquired the White Star Line from the Inte national Mercantile Marine Company they withdrew their North Atlan service, and transferred the *Ohio* to the White Star Line, again renamed *Albert* She was placed on the Liverpool–Quebec and Montreal route and proved ve popular in that trade. During the post war emigration boom she carri thousands of passengers to Canada. In March, 1933, she was laid up on t Clyde, and in 1934 was sold to Japanese shipbreakers, for scrapping. A sh life for such a fine and popular vessel.

ALBERTIC

No. 46. GREAT EASTERN. 1857

(Ex. Leviathan)

OWNERS: Eastern & Occidental S.S. Company.

SERVICE: (Intended) London and Far East.

NAT. & PORT: British. London.

BUILDERS: Scott, Russell & Co., Millwall, London, 1857.

TONNAGE: 18,914 tons gross.

DIMENSIONS: 680 ft. lg. o.a. x 80 ft. beam.

ENGINES: 2 paddle wheels and single screw. She had 8 driving engines on her paddle and screw shafts. 3,675 h.p. on her paddle, 7,675 h.p. on her screw propeller. By Boulton, Watt & Co.
Coal consumption 300 tons per day. Bunkers for 10,000 tons.

The largest vessel built until the *Celtic* of 1902, and known as Brunel's gigantic failure. The ship was designed too far ahead of the craft of the mechanical and steam engineers. The idea behind her design was to enable a steamer to trade to the Far East, carrying enough coal for the return trip, with the result that there was very little room for anything else.

Brunel decided to launch her broadside on, and when the launch commenced, Brunel, fearing she might take the water too suddenly, ordered her to be checked, with the result that she stuck, and was not finally afloat until three months later. The company who had ordered her, in the meantime, went insolvent. She was later bought by a company who intended to run her on the Atlantic, but she was a failure.

Her most successful venture was in 1866 when she laid the first Atlantic cable connecting the British Isles with North America. After this success she was laid up and eventually was sent round the coast as an exhibition and show ship, being finally laid up in the Mersey. In 1885 she was being taken to be broken up when she went aground, and was finally broken up in 1887.

Although a colossal failure she was the forerunner of the giant steamships of to-day, and, if Brunel had only had more efficient engines, no doubt she would have proved her worth.

GREAT EASTERN

No. 47. LAPLAND. 1909

OWNERS:	The Red Star Line. International M.M. Company. Registered by F. Leyland & Co., Ltd., Liverpool.
SERVICE:	Antwerp–New York, and Cruising.
NAT. & PORT:	British. Liverpool.
BUILDERS:	Harland & Wolff, Ltd., Belfast, 1909.
TONNAGE:	18,864 tons gross.
DIMENSIONS:	605·8 ft. lg. o.a. x 70·4 ft. beam x 37·4 ft. depth. Drt. 32 ft. 1 in. 5 decks.
ENGINES:	2 quadruple expansion steam engines. 16,000 s.h.p. Twin screw. Normal speed 16 knots.
BOILERS:	8 D.E. boilers. F. D. stm. pr. 215 lbs. per square inch.
PAINTWORK:	Hull black with red band, upper works white, funnels black with white band and black top.
COMPLEMENT:	1,200 passengers, 370 officers and crew.

A great carrier of emigrants and a fine luxurious ship of her day, popular with regular travellers. She had a straight stem and counter stern, with two funnels and four masts, similar to the White Star liners of that period. She did useful service in the war, both as a troopship and munition and food ship. Latterly she was employed mostly on cruising, and in 1933 sailed nearly 30,000 miles on cruises, calling at over fifty ports. She was laid up when her repair and overhaul costs were getting too high, and in November, 1933, was sold to Japanese shipbreakers for approximately £30,000 as she lay at Antwerp.

[By courtesy of the International M.M. Comp.

LAPLAND

No. 48. CONTE VERDE. 1923

OWNERS:	Lloyd-Triestino. " Italia " Line.
SERVICE:	Trieste–New York, later transferred to Italy–India, China and Japan service.
NAT. & PORT:	Italian. Genoa.
BUILDERS:	Sir Wm. Beardmore & Co., Ltd., Glasgow, 1923.
TONNAGE:	18,765 tons gross.
DIMENSIONS:	570·2 ft. lg. b.p. x 74 ft. beam x 35·9 ft. depth. 5 decks.
ENGINES:	4 steam tubrines, d.r. geared to 2 screw shafts. 21,000 s.h.p. Twin screw. Normal speed 20 knots.
BOILERS:	6 D.E. and 2 S.E. boilers, 200 lbs. F. D.
PAINTWORK:	Hull white with blue band round, boot-topping green, upper works white, funnels buff.
COMPLEMENT:	208 first class, 268 cabin class and 1,880 third class passengers.

Sister ship to *Conte Rosso*.

A pair of fine steamers of intermediate size and good speed. This vessel is one of the last liners to be built in Great Britain for Italy; since this date Italy has not only become an owner of large liners but a builder of big ships too, not only for Italian lines but for foreign shipowners as well, as for instance the two Polish-American Line ships lately built in Italy for the North Atlantic, each of 14,400 tons, and named *Pilsudski* and *Batory*.

[By courtesy of Italia Line

CONTE VERDE

No. 49. LAURENTIC. 1927

OWNERS:	Cunard White Star Line.
SERVICE:	Liverpool–Quebec and Boston, and Cruising.
NAT. & PORT:	British. Liverpool.
BUILDERS:	Harland & Wolff, Ltd., Belfast, 1927.
TONNAGE:	18,724 tons gross.
DIMENSIONS:	578·2 ft. lg. b.p. x 75·4 ft. beam x 40 ft. depth. 5 decks.
ENGINES:	2 4 cyl. trip. exp. engines and 1 low pressure turbine. 15,000 s.h.p. Triple screw. Normal speed 16 knots.
PAINTWORK:	Hull black with gold band, boot-topping red, upper works white, funnels buff with black tops.
COMPLEMENT:	1,600 passengers.

Her first Captain was Capt. E. L. Trant, R.D., R.N.R., who became Commander of the *Majestic* and Commodore of the White Star Fleet.

A fine example of intermediate class liner, very popular on Canadian and Boston trades, and a famous cruising ship. With a straight stem, cruiser stern, two masts and two funnels, she had a good appearance. Named after an earlier ship of the same line which was wrecked at the entrance to Lough Swilley, Co. Donegal, Ireland, in 1917, with £5,000,000 worth of gold on board. In October, 1932, she left Liverpool for Quebec equipped as an Exhibition Ship, displaying goods of British manufacture, in connexion with the Ottawa Empire Conference.

On Oct. 3rd, 1932, when on voyage from Quebec to Liverpool she was in collision with the Belfast steamship *Lurigethan*, sixteen miles east of Point Amour at the western entrance to Belle Isle Strait, in a fog. Both steamers were damaged above the water line, but proceeded on their voyages.

In March, 1934, she left Dublin for Italy with seven hundred pilgrims on board to witness the ceremony of closing the Holy Door in Saint Peter's Cathedral in Rome, by His Holiness the Pope, on Easter Monday. Ten altars were fitted in the ship and many priests were on board, a cinema was also fitted for entertainments during the voyage.

On Sunday, Aug. 18th, 1935, when outward bound from Liverpool on a cruise to Northern Ports with 620 passengers on board, she was in collision with the Blue Star liner *Napier Star*, of London, in a fog in the Irish Sea. Six members of the crew were killed—crushed to death by the impact as they lay asleep in their berths, five others being seriously injured.

The *Napier Star* ripped a great hole in the starboard bow of the *Laurentic*, smashing in twelve of the crew's cabins in the forecastle head.

The *Laurentic* had only left Liverpool on the Saturday evening and had only been at sea for four hours when the crash occurred which rudely awakened

LAURENTIC

the passengers to horror and tragedy, the passengers were ordered to don their life-jackets and they rushed on deck, the crew ordered everybody to remain calm as there was no danger, confidence was quickly restored and there was no panic.

The ship returned to Liverpool for repairs and the passengers were transferred to the *Lancastria* and the *Homeric*.

In Dec., 1935, she was laid up and it was freely rumoured towards the end of the year that she was to be sold.

In Oct., 1935, an enquiry was opened on the collision with the *Napier Star*.

In Jan., 1936, the Admiralty Court sitting on the mishap found that both vessels were equally to blame for the collision.

1936, Sept. Was commissioned as troopship for transport of troops to Palestine.

1936, Sept. 14th. Left Southampton with troops for Palestine.

No. 50. CAP TRAFALGAR. 1914

OWNERS:	The Hamburg South American Line (H.S.D.G.).
SERVICE:	Hamburg, Vigo, Lisbon, Madeira, Bahia, Rio, Buenos Ayres.
NAT. & PORT:	German. Hamburg.
BUILDERS:	Vulkan Werke, Hamburg, 1914.
TONNAGE:	18,509 tons gross.
DIMENSIONS:	590 ft. lg. x 72 ft. beam x 42 ft. depth. 5 passenger decks.
ENGINES:	2 sets of 4 cyl. trip. exp. steam engines on outer shafts, and one L.P. turbine on centre shaft. 15,150 i.h.p. Triple screw. Normal speed 17 knots.
PAINTWORK:	Hull black with red boot-topping, upper works white, funnels white with red tops.

Flagship of the H.S.D.G. Fleet.

The largest liner sailing to South America to date. This great and beautiful ship was one of the most luxurious vessels to cross the Equator; owing to the fortunes of war, she, however, only made one complete round trip, in the early part of the summer of 1914.

1914, March. Made her acceptance trials.

1914, July. Capt. Walter H. Parker, C.B.E., R.D., R.N.R., Retd., late Commander of the *Olympic*, states in his excellent book, *Leaves from an Unwritten Log-Book*, that when in Buenos Aires in July, 1914, with his *Pardo* the *Cap Trafalgar* arrived in the Darsena Norte on her second voyage, "I had paid particular attention to her outward appearance on her first voyage, therefore immediately noticed that, in addition to the ordinary look-out crow's nest on the foremast, a lofty mast-head one had been fitted! Which in view of the European crisis that had arisen during the last few weeks, had to me a sinister significance. The feverish coaling operations on a large scale engaged in fore and aft immediately after her arrival, confirmed my private opinion that she was secretly armed, and could be quickly converted into an auxiliary cruiser.

"After the declaration of war, she cleared (we were told) for Las Palmas. The next thing we heard, less than a month later, was that she had turned up at Montevideo to coal again; the question arose as to what had become of the coal she had left Buenos Aires with, as she was reported to have no less than 1,500 tons on board on turning up at Montevideo. It was rightly considered more than suspicious, nevertheless she got what she wanted, and it may be taken that the intelligence was promptly cabled to London. By this time, of course, England was well into the war; several armed raiders, or enemy war-ships, were reported in the Atlantic. We could only surmise that *Cap Trafalgar's* surplus coal had been transferred to one or the other of these under cover of darkness."

In August the Cunarder *Carmania* arriving at Liverpool from New York was speedily prepared for duty as an armed merchant-cruiser and immediately

CAP TRAFALGAR

ent out to search for enemy raiders. On Sept. 14th, when off Trinidad, she ighted the *Cap Trafalgar* and immediately engaged her in action. Both ships withheld their fire until the range had closed to 7,500 yards, and it was not until the range had closed to 3,500 that the *Cap Trafalgar* turned away. But he *Cap Trafalgar* was so badly damaged that she sank in two hours after the first gun had been fired. The fact that her hull had been sub-divided longitudinally has been held to account for her sudden sinking. *Carmania* too was badly damaged, having been hit by no fewer than seventy-nine direct hits, but managed to reach port. This was the first gun action fought between two merchant cruisers, and t proved the unsuitability of passenger liners for this service, having no protection for their high freeboard and high superstructures. It has also been said hat when the action ceased *Carmania* was so badly damaged that the whole of her bridge controls were out of action, and when it is remembered that all the vital controls of a liner are centred on the bridge, it will be realised what this might have meant. The crews, however, of both ships fought splendidly.

No. 51. CERAMIC. 1913

OWNERS: Shaw, Savill & Albion Line.
SERVICE: London–Australia and New Zealand.
NAT. & PORT: British. Liverpool.
BUILDERS: Harland & Wolff, Ltd., Belfast, 1913.
TONNAGE: 18,495 tons gross.
DIMENSIONS: 655·1 ft. lg. o.a. x 69·4 ft. beam x 43·8 ft. depth. 4 passenger decks.
ENGINES: 2 quadruple expansion engines on outside shafts and one low pressure turbine on centre chaft. Triple screw. Normal speed 16 knots.
PAINTWORK: Hull black with white band, boot-topping red, upper works white funnel buff with black top.
COMPLEMENT: 336 passengers. Officers and crew 260.

A fine-looking ship with four masts and one funnel, like many Harland & Wolff ships, she is noted for her big cargo carrying capacity and for bringing big Christmas cargoes to London. Built for the Australian via Cape service of the White Star Line. In 1934 she was sold with the other White Star Line Australian trade interests to the Shaw, Savill & Albion Line, which previous to the amalgamation of the Cunard and White Star Line's Atlantic fleets had been an associated company. She has now been sold with the Shaw Savill fleet to Messrs Furness Withy & Company of London.

1936. Considerable alterations to her accommodation and machinery were made by Messrs. Harland & Wolff, Ltd., at their Glasgow shipyard. All the public rooms have been re-decorated, a gymnasium and a large verandah café added. A thousand men were employed on the job.

Capt. R. J. Noal, Marine Superintendent of the Line, was responsible for the alterations.

1936, Aug. Capt. T. E. Musgrave, who was once in command of her, died. He had a very distinguished career, commencing in sail with the firm of Messrs Edward Bates & Sons, of Liverpool. His first command was the White Star liner *Cufic* and in 1917 was in command of the *Southland* when she was torpedoed and sunk. He also commanded the American Line's *Haverford* when she made two historic landings of troops at Gallipoli. Another ship he commanded was the *Suevic*.

1936, Aug. 22nd. She left Liverpool for New Zealand via the Cape, calling at Durban as well as Capetown.

CERAMIC

[By courtesy of Cunard White Star Line]

No. 52. EMPRESS OF FRANCE. 1914

(Ex. Alsatian)

OWNERS:	The Canadian Pacific S.S. Ltd.
SERVICE:	Southampton–Quebec and Halifax, and Cruising.
NAT. & PORT:	British. London.
BUILDERS:	Sir Wm. Beardmore & Co., Ltd., Glasgow, 1914.
TONNAGE:	18,487 tons gross. 10,747 tons nett.
DIMENSIONS:	571·4 ft. lg. b.p. x 72·4 ft. beam x 41·7 ft. depth. 5 decks.
ENGINES:	4 sets of steam turbines. 21,000 s.h.p. Quadruple screw. Normal speed 20 knots.
BOILERS:	6 D.E. and 4 S.E. boilers. Coal-fired, with coal consumption of 275 tons per day.
PAINTWORK:	Hull white with blue band round, boot-topping green, upper works white, funnels buff.
COMPLEMENT:	1,500 passengers. 725 officers and crew.

Built for the Allan Line as the *Alsatian* and was the finest and fastest liner to be built before the war for the Canadian trade; she was the first liner to have motor lifeboats and the first Atlantic liner with a cruiser stern. Her accommodation with splendid public rooms and de-luxe staterooms and suites was in line with the New York Express mail liners, and she soon acquired a reputation on the service. First Canadian liner with a speed of 20 knots.

1913, March 22nd. Launched.

1914, Jan. 17th. Commenced maiden voyage, Capt. Edmund Outram, Liverpool to Halifax.

1914, Aug. Commissioned as armed auxiliary cruiser, and became the flagship of the famous 10th Cruiser Squadron. Rescued crew of auxiliary cruiser *Oceanic* (White Star Line).

1918, May. Had collision with Cunarder *Ausonia* in Mersey.

1918, Dec. Released from her commission during which she had steamed 266,700 nautical miles, and had examined 15,000 ships.

1919, Jan. 17th. She left the Mersey for the Clyde for refit. She was entirely modernised and renamed as above, being then placed on the Liverpool–Quebec service, and carried the Duke and Duchess of Devonshire to Canada on the appointment of the Duke as Governor-General (Capt. Cook in command).

1920. Made record passage for Canadian run of 5 days 23 hrs., and shortly after made round trip in 15 days 5 hrs. 5 mins.

1921. Transferred to Southampton–Quebec service.

1922. Inaugurated C.P.R. Co's. Quebec, Cherbourg, Southampton and Hamburg service.

1923. Made a number of successful cruises. She was selected to carry H.R.H. Prince Edward to Canada. Later again re-fitted and converted to oil burning.

1931. She was laid up in the Clyde.

1934, Oct. Sold to Glasgow scrappers for about £35,000.

[By courtesy of Canadian Pacific S.S., Ltd.

EMPRESS OF FRANCE

No. 53. CALGARIAN. 1913

OWNERS: The Canadian Pacific Steamships, Ltd.

SERVICE: Liverpool–Quebec.

NAT. & PORT: British. Glasgow.

BUILDERS: The Fairfield Shipbuilding & Engineering Co., Ltd., Glasgow, 1913

TONNAGE: 18,481 tons gross.

DIMENSIONS: 571·4 ft. lg. b.p. x 72·4 ft. beam x 41·7 ft. depth. 5 decks.

ENGINES: 4 sets of Parsons steam turbines. 21,000 s.h.p. Quadruple screw Normal speed 19 knots.

BOILERS: 6 D.E. and 4 S.E. boilers. Coal consumption, 275 tons per day.

PAINTWORK: Hull black with white band, boot-topping green, upper works white funnels buff.

COMPLEMENT: 1,500 passengers and 750 officers and crew.

Sister ship to the famous *Empress of France*, ex *Alsatian*. The finest and fastes pre-war liners to Canada.

1914, Aug. Was commissioned as an auxiliary cruiser, blockaded mouth River Tagus with H.M.A.S. *Sydney*.

1916. Sold with Allan Line Fleet to the Canadian Pacific Railway Compan (C.P.S.S. Ltd.).

1918, March 1st. When on convoy duty she was sunk by four torpedoe forty-nine lives were lost.

CALGARIAN

No. 54. DE GRASSE. 1924

OWNERS:	Cie. Generale Transatlantique. (The French Line.)
SERVICE:	Havre and West Indies.
NAT. & PORT:	French. Havre.
BUILDERS:	Cammell Laird & Co., Ltd., Birkenhead, 1924.
TONNAGE:	18,435 tons gross.
DIMENSIONS:	571 ft. lg. o.a. x 72 ft. beam x 42 ft. depth. 5 decks.
ENGINES:	4 steam turbines, S.R. geared to 2 shafts. 16,000 s.h.p. Twin screw. Normal speed 16 knots.
PAINTWORK:	Hull black, boot-topping red, upper works white, funnels red with black top.
COMPLEMENT:	535 cabin class passengers.

Named after one of the noblest gentlemen of France.

A "roomy" ship of "Boulevard" decks and out-door "great open spaces," she is another bit of France and a very popular one, combines that homelike feeling with real artistic charm. During a trip round her decks one would get a glimpse of her vast terrace café, with its bright coloured wicker chairs and tables, the chummy gallery, a favourite spot for quiet letter writing, the Library and children's play room. The grand salon is a regal yet restful room with tapestried furniture and inlaid woods. To sum up she is a fine example of modern liner of intermediate size.

DE GRASSE

No. 55. VIRGINIA. 1928

OWNERS:	American Line S.S. Corp., Panama-Pacific Line.
SERVICE:	New York–San Francisco.
NAT. & PORT:	United States. New York.
BUILDERS:	Newport News S.B. & D.D. Co., Newport News, Va., U.S., 1928.
TONNAGE:	18,298 tons gross.
DIMENSIONS:	613 ft. lg. o.a., 586·4 ft. lg. b.p. x 80·3 ft. beam x 42 ft. depth. Drt. 32 ft. 5 decks.
ENGINES:	2 steam turbine-generators ea. 6,600 k.w., 2,880 r.p.m., 4,000 volt 3 ph. 2 electric motors on shafts, ea. 8,500 s.h.p., 120 r.p.m. By General Electric Co., Schentady, N.Y. Twin screw. Normal speed 18 knots.
BOILERS:	8 Babcock & Wilcocks water tube, 300 lbs. stm. pr. 200 deg. F. S.H. Oil fuel.
PAINTWORK:	Hull black, boot-topping red, upper works white, funnels red with blue tops and white band.
COMPLEMENT:	409 1st, 330 tourist class passengers.

Sister ships *Pennsylvania* and *California*. The three sister ships provide a fortnightly service from New York.

The second of the three sister ships, which were the first large liners to have turbo-electric drive making an historic step in marine propulsion. This drive has been so successful that other companies soon followed the example culminating in the decision of the French Line to install similar equipment in the great *Normandie*. The *Virginia* entered service in 1928 shortly after the *California*. The accommodation is very beautiful and artistic and all the refinements of the big express liners are found.

[*By courtesy of the Panama-Pacific Line*

VIRGINIA

No. 56. PENNSYLVANIA. 1928

OWNERS:	American Line S.S. Corp., Panama-Pacific Line.
SERVICE:	New York–San Francisco.
NAT. & PORT:	United States. New York.
BUILDERS:	Newport News S.B. & D.D. Co., Newport News., Va., U.S., 1928.
TONNAGE:	18,200 tons gross.
DIMENSIONS:	613 ft. lg. o.a., 586·4 ft. lg. b.p. x 80·3 ft. beam x 42·5 ft. depth. Drt. 34·5 ft. 5 decks.
ENGINES:	2 steam turbine-generators 6,600 k.w., 4,000 volt., 2 electric motors on screw shafts, 17,000 s.h.p. synchronous induction, 4,000 volt, 120 r.p.m. Twin screw. Normal speed 18 knots.
BOILERS:	8 Babcock & Wilcocks water tube, 300 lbs. stm. pr. 200 deg. S.H. Oil fuel.
EL. LT. & PWR.:	4 G.E.C. turbo-genrs., 3 wire 500 k.w., 120/240 volt.
PAINTWORK:	Hull black, boot-topping red, white upper works, funnel red with blue top and white band.
COMPLEMENT:	471 1st class, 334 tourist class passengers.

Sister ships *Virginia* and *California*.

The third of these fine ships which have proved so popular on the American inter-coastal service via the Panama Canal.

[*By courtesy of Panama-Pacific Line*

PENNSYLVANIA

No. 57. SCHARNHORST. 1935

OWNERS:	The North German Lloyd Company.
SERVICE:	Bremen–Dover and the Far East.
NAT. & PORT:	German. Bremen.
BUILDERS:	The Weser Shipbuilding Company, Bremen, 1935.
TONNAGE:	18,194 tons gross.
DIMENSIONS:	652 ft. lg. o.a., 610·75 ft. lg. b.p. x 73·8 ft. beam x 45 ft. depth. 5 passenger decks.
ENGINES:	2 steam turbine-generators each 10,000 k.w. capacity at 3,120 r.p.m., 3,120 volts. 3 phase. 2 electric shaft motors each of 13,000 s.h.p. Twin screw. Normal speed 20 knots.
BOILERS:	4 single water tube boilers, steam pressure 710 lbs. per sq. in. super-heated to 878 degrees F. Oil fuel.
PAINTWORK:	Hull black with white line dividing red boot-topping, upper works white, funnel buff.
COMPLEMENT:	152 1st, 144 2nd class passengers.

The first German turbo-electric liner and the largest Maierform ship in the world. A fine example of a modern intermediate liner, the accommodation is equal to the famous express liners on the Atlantic trade. Another notable point is the high steam pressure used.

Sister ships *Gneisenau* and *Potsdam*.

1935, May. On trials, made 21 knots on measured mile.

1935, May 10th. Left Bremen on her maiden voyage; arrived back at Bremen late and her next sailing was postponed.

SCHARNHORST

[By courtesy of Norddeutscher Lloyd Line

No. 58. LURLINE. 1932

OWNERS:	The Matson Line, Oceanic Steamship Company, San Francisco.
SERVICE:	San Francisco–Los Angeles, to Honolulu.
NAT. & PORT:	United States. San Francisco.
BUILDERS:	The Bethlehem Shipbuilding Corporation, Quincy, Mass., U.S.A., 1932.
TONNAGE:	18,021 tons gross.
DIMENSIONS:	632 ft. lg. o.a. x 79 ft. beam. 6 decks.
ENGINES:	6 steam turbines, single reduction geared to 2 screw shafts, 22,000 s.h.p. Twin screw. Normal speed 20½ knots.
BOILERS:	12 water tube boilers, stm. pr. 400 lbs. F.D. Oil fuel.
PAINTWORK:	Hull and upper works white, boot-topping green, funnels buff with blue tops.
COMPLEMENT:	700 passengers in saloon and cabin classes. 350 officers and crew.
REMARKS:	18 large lifeboats are carried in patent davits.

Sister ship to *Monterey* and *Mariposa*.

A beautiful example of modern craftsmanship in build and design, especially built for tropical travel. With her sister ships they are the first large liners to have their entire sides heavily insulated with a cork lining to exclude the heat of the sun in tropical climes. Every six minutes the air in every stateroom is automatically changed, the passenger controlling at will a noiseless system of ventilation. The dining saloons have an air-conditioning system which regulates not only the temperature but the humidity as well. Both dining saloons are situated on "E" deck, the 1st class saloon being amidships between the funnel uptakes, and the cabin class saloon further aft.

The 1st class dining saloon is a gorgeous room with brilliant murals by Paul Arnat, capturing the spirit of the sea in original vistas of old-time ships and palm fringed isles.

Every 1st class stateroom has full length mirrors, wardrobes, dressing tables, ice water thermos bottles, electric fans, ample baggage space, private telephone and private bath and toilet.

The lounge is unusually large and decorated with restrained smartness and unusual artistry. The smoke room is a fascinating room equipped with a bar close to hand. There are also men's club room, from which ladies are excluded; quiet library; and a gay verandah café-Bohemia; capital gymnasium; deck tennis courts; clay pigeon shooting; two large swimming pools and children's play rooms.

LURLINE

[By courtesy of the Matson-Oceanic Line

No. 59. MARIPOSA. 1931

OWNERS:	Oceanic Steamship Co. The Matson Line.
SERVICE:	San Francisco–Australia and New Zealand via Honolulu.
NAT. & PORT:	United States. San Francisco.
BUILDERS:	Bethlehem Shipbuilding Corporation, Quincy, Mass., U.S.A., 1931.
TONNAGE:	18,017 tons gross.
DIMENSIONS:	632 ft. lg. o.a. x 79 ft. beam. 6 passenger decks.
ENGINES:	6 steam turbines, single reduction geared to 2 screw shafts, 22,000 s.h.p. Twin screw. Normal speed 20½ knots.
BOILERS:	12 water tube boilers, stm. pr. 400 lbs. F.D. Oil fuel.
PAINTWORK:	Hull and upper works white, boot-topping green, funnels buff with blue tops.
COMPLEMENT:	700 passengers in saloon and cabin class. 350 officers and crew.
REMARKS:	18 lifeboats carried on patent davits.

The three sister ships *Lurline, Monterey* and *Mariposa* are noted for luxurious travel through semi-tropical seas. Every appliance known for the safety and comfort of passengers and for dependability has been installed, and they combine the last word in advanced marine engineering construction with the highest standards of comfort. Tailor shops, Beauty parlours, Barbers' shops, electric elevators and cargo winches, novelty shops, Photographic dark rooms for passengers' use, daily newspapers together with a twenty-four hour service combine to make passengers forget that they are at sea.

They are noted for the spacious comfort of their cabin class accommodation which offers the tourist a new standard of travel.

Eight of the de-luxe suites have private verandah decks with more than one hundred square feet of teak covered open deck space.

Each has a cargo capacity of 5,000 tons and have large side ports for handling cargo in or out of the holds, four hatchways and ten of the world's fastest cargo winches; these electric cargo winches have all gearing running in oil, and are so silent in operation that passengers are not disturbed when cargo is being handled at intermediate ports.

The three liners cost over twenty-four million dollars.

On trials the *Mariposa* did 21.3 knots on a displacement of 23,000 tons, propeller speed of 125 r.p.m.

MARIPOSA

[By courtesy of the Matson-Oceanic Line

No. 60. MONTEREY. 1932

OWNERS:	Oceanic Steamship Company, Matson Line.
SERVICE:	San Francisco–Australia–New Zealand via Honolulu.
NAT. & PORT:	United States, San Francisco.
BUILDERS:	The Bethlehem Shipbuilding Corporation, Quincy, Mass., U.S.A., 1932.
TONNAGE:	18,017 tons gross.
DIMENSIONS:	632 ft. lg. o.a. x 79 ft. beam. 6 passenger decks.
ENGINES:	6 steam turbines, single reduction geared to 2 screw shafts, 22,000 s.h.p. Twin screw. Normal speed 20½ knots.
BOILERS:	12 water tube boilers, stm. pr. 400 lbs. F.D. Oil fuel.
EL. LT. & PWR.:	Plant is equal to that provided for an American city of 25,000 population.
PAINTWORK:	Hull and upper works white, boot-topping green, funnels buff with blue tops.
COMPLEMENT:	420 passengers in saloon, 158 passengers in cabin class. 350 officers and crew.

With her sister ships *Lurline* and *Mariposa* these fine Pacific liners have all the refinements and luxury of the finest of the Atlantic liners.

All auxiliary machinery and cargo winches, etc., are electrically operated. Each ship has sixteen watertight compartments and seven fireproof divisions, each fitted with automatic fire alarm system.

Each cargo space and storage room is protected by a carbon dioxide fire extinguishing system controlled from the chart house. Eighteen lifeboats are carried on patent davits to facilitate lowering.

MONTEREY

[By courtesy of the Matson–Oceanic Line

No. 61. GNEISENAU. 1935

Owners:	The North German Lloyd.
Service:	Bremen-Southampton, Far East.
Nat. & Port	German. Bremen.
Builders:	The Deutsche Schiff-und Maschinenbau, A.G., Bremen, 1935.
Tonnage:	18,000 tons gross.
Dimensions:	652 ft. lg. o.a., 610·75 ft. lg. b.p. x 73·8 ft. beam. x 45 ft. depth. 5 passenger decks.
Engines:	2 sets of steam turbines, sin. red. geared. 26,000 s.h.p. Twin screw. Normal speed 20 knots.
Boilers:	4 single water tube boilers, stm. pr. 710 lbs. per sq. in., superheated to 878 deg. F. superheat. Oil fuel.
Paintwork:	Hull black with white line dividing red boot-topping, upper works white, funnel buff.
Complement:	152 1st class and 144 tourist class passengers.
Remarks:	Cargo capacity 10,800 tons.

With her sister ship *Scharnhorst* she is the largest Maierform ship completed up to date.

Another sister ship in all except hull form and machinery is the *Potsdam*.

The advent of these three fine liners, the finest German ships on the Eastern run, has enabled the Norddeutscher Lloyd to re-open their pre-war routes in the Far East.

They are beautifully modern in the design and artistic taste of the passenger accommodation and are splendidly equipped vessels, both for the passengers' comfort and safety.

A notable feature is the large open air swimming bath and almost every stateroom has a private bath.

The great curved Maierform bow can be readily seen in the illustration and another noticeable feature is the safety valve steam pipes which it will be seen are carried up the inside of the funnel casing.

The three ships are scheduled to cover the trip from Genoa to Shanghai in twenty-three days.

1935, May 17th. Launched.

GNEISENAU

No. 62. PRESIDENT LINCOLN. 1903

(Ex. Scotian)

OWNERS:	U.S. Government.
SERVICE:	North Atlantic Transport.
NAT. & PORT:	United States. New York.
BUILDERS:	Harland & Wolff, Ltd., Belfast, 1903.
TONNAGE:	18,074 tons gross.
DIMENSIONS:	599 ft. lg. o.a. x 68·2 ft. beam x 48 ft. depth. 5 passenger decks.
ENGINES:	2 quadruple expansion 4 cyl. engines, 6,000 s.h.p. Twin screw. Normal speed 13½ knots.

With her sister ship *President Grant*, ex *Servian*, which became the *Republic* of the United States Lines, these two fine vessels were noted for being the only six-masted liners on the Atlantic. They had very large accommodation for emigrants and big cargo space. They proved very useful transports during the war.

1903. Built for Messrs. Furness Withy & Company, Ltd., London, and named *Scotian*, for the North Atlantic trade, but with her sister ship the *Servian* was sold to the Hamburg–Amerika Line and re-named *President Lincoln*, her sister being re-named *President Grant*.

They were very successful ships of their class and while not in the spectacular class they were big profit earners.

1914, Aug. Interned in the United States.

1917. Seized by the United States Government and converted into transport.

1918, May 31st. Torpedoed and sunk.

[*Photo: Nautical Photo Agency*

PRESIDENT LINCOLN

STATISTICS AND HISTORIES

STATISTICS OF THE LINERS

NATIONALITY

British	37
United States . . .	9
German	8
Italian	4
Dutch	2
French	1
Swedish	1
	—
	62

ENGINES

Steam Turbines	27
Motor Engines . . .	9
Turbine-Electric	8
Quad. Expansion engines . .	8
Triple Expansion engines . .	1
Reciprocating and Turbine . .	6
Reciprocating with Bauer-Wach exhaust turbines	2
Simple engines	1
	62
	—

BUILDERS OF THE LINERS

Harland & Wolff	13
John Brown & Co., Ltd. . .	8
Vickers, Ltd.	6
Herrin Blohm & Voss, Hamburg .	4
Vulcan Werkes, Germany . .	4
Sir Wm. Beardmore & Co., Ltd. .	3
Weser Yard, Bremen . . .	2
Bethlehem S.B. Corp., U.S.A. . .	3
Cammell Laird & Co., Ltd. . .	2
Newport News S.B. Co., U.S.A. .	2
Nederland S.B. Co., Holland . .	2
Cantieri Reuniti, Italy . . .	2
Teckleburgs, Danzig . . .	2
Swan, Hunter & Wigham Richardson, Ltd.	2
Fairfield S.B. & Eng. Co., Ltd. .	2
Eastern Shipbuilding Corp., U.S.A. .	1
Workman, Clarke & Co., Ltd. .	1
Scott Russell, London . . .	1
Alex. Stephen & Sons, Ltd. . .	1
Deutsche Schiff-und Masch. A.G., Bremen	1
	62
	—

NUMBER OF PROPELLERS PER SHIP

One and Paddles	1
Twin screw	48
Triple screw	7
Quadruple screw	6
	62
	—

NUMBERS OF FUNNELS, PER SHIP

Five funnels	1
Four ,, ...	6
Three ,, ...	6
Two ,, ...	36
One funnel	13
	62
	—

OWNERS OF THE LINERS

Cunard White Star Line. . .	11
Canadian Pacific Line . . .	8
Union Castle Line . . .	5
Orient Line	5
Hamburg–Amerika Line . .	4
Italia Lines	4
P. & O. S.N. Co. . . .	3
Matson Line	3
Atlantic Transport Line . . .	2
American Line Corporation . .	2
Nederland Line	2
Norddeutscher Lloyd . . .	2
Hamburg Sud-Amerika Line .	2

Furness Withy & Co. . . .	1
Shaw, Savill & Albion Line . .	1
Swedish America Line . . .	1
Red Star Line	1
French Line	1
Eastern S.S. Co.	1
U.S. Government	1
U.S. Shipping Board . . .	1
U.S. Navy Dept.	1
	62
	—

The Cunard White Star includes the present Cunard White Star Line, the White Star Line and the Cunard S.S. Co., Ltd.

The following lines have now ceased to trade:

    The Atlantic Transport Line

    Eastern S.S. Co.

HISTORIES OF SOME FAMOUS BRITISH SHIPPING LINES

THE CANADIAN PACIFIC STEAMSHIPS, LTD.

Fleet, 18 steamships. Totalling approximately 325,000 tons gross.
President of the Canadian Pacific Railway Company: Sir Edward W. Beatty.

This great line of Atlantic and Pacific Ocean steamships is the ocean steamship department of the Canadian Pacific Railway Company, which great company, one of the greatest transport concerns in the British Empire, finally bridging Canada with the iron road, in the year 1887 began to charter steamers for trade on the Pacific to feed its transcontinental railway lines.

The first vessels chartered were the ex-Cunard liners *Abyssinia* of 1870, 3,376 tons, *Batavia* and *Parthia* of the same year, the latter ship being the first Cunarder to be fitted with compound engines.

These vessels were placed on the Vancouver–Orient route, and in 1889 the Company received from the Postmaster-General a contract for mails on what had become known as the "All Red Route," that is from England to Halifax, N.S., thence to Vancouver by train and from there to Hong Kong by steamer.

To meet the terms of this contract three fine vessels, which became world-famous were built, *Empress of China*, *Empress of India* and *Empress of Japan*, each of 5,800 tons gross, with a normal average speed of 16½ knots. They were beautiful vessels with graceful lines and clipper stems. In 1913 two new vessels, the *Empress of Russia* and the *Empress of Asia*, were built, each of 17,000 tons, with triple screws driven by steam turbines. In 1922 a third fine mail steamer was put in service, the *Empress of Canada*, of 21,517 tons. Other steamers were employed on the Pacific Ocean in addition to the mail steamers.

On the Atlantic Ocean the Company did not enter into competition with existing lines, but in 1903 they bought the Beaver Line from Elder Dempster & Co. This line was old in the Canadian trade, having been established in the 1850's with sailing ships, and had later operated a fine fleet of steamers.

The Canadian Pacific Line immediately added some fine ships to the fleet, the most notable of which were the *Empress of Britain* and the *Empress of Ireland* of 1905. These two fine ships were great competitors of the Allan Line's crack ships *Victorian* and *Virginian*.

Competition between the two lines became very keen, and in 1915 the Canadian Pacific Railway Company absorbed the older and rival Allan Line with its fleet of thirty-nine ships, totalling approximately 400,000 tons gross.

After the Armistice the Canadian Pacific Line commenced to replace its war losses and started operations to improve the Atlantic, Pacific and Canadian Coastal and Lakes services.

The fine cabin class liners, *Montcalm*, *Montclare* and *Montrose*, were added to the Atlantic fleet, three ex-German liners were bought and re-named *Empress of Scotland*, *Empress of China*—now known as *Empress of Australia*—and *Montreal*.

For the Pacific run the *Empress of Canada* was built in 1922 and another ex-German liner was purchased and renamed *Empress of Australia*. The ex-Allan liner *Alsatian* was renamed *Empress of France*.

The four fine Duchess class steamers were added to the Atlantic fleet in 1928–9 and put on the Liverpool–Quebec run, and five big cargo vessels, known as the "Beaver" boats, perhaps the finest cargo vessels afloat, were built and put on the London and Quebec service about the same time.

For the Pacific fleet another big fine ship was built in 1930 and named *Empress of Japan*, and following her was the great *Empress of Britain*, known as Britain's wonder ship, she was the largest vessel built in the British Isles since the *Britannic* of 1914.

The Canadian Pacific Railway Company operates the great trans-continental railway from Halifax to Vancouver, Atlantic and Pacific Liners, Canadian Coastal, River and Lake steamers and many hotels, and is the greatest travel organisation in the world.

THE CUNARD WHITE STAR LINE

Chairman: Sir Percy Bates.

Present fleet, 20 vessels.   Approximate total tonnage 531,728 tons gross.

This Company was formed in January, 1934, by the merger of the Atlantic fleets and interests of those two historic companies, the Cunard Steamship Company, Ltd., and the White Star Line, Ltd.

The merger was the outcome of negotiations instigated at the request of the Government when approached for financial assistance for the completion of the *Queen Mary*. The new company, with a fleet of over 500,000 tons, the largest fleet on the North Atlantic Ocean, thus brings under single control the two famous fleets which for nearly a century have built up a service world renowned for its efficiency.

The Cunard Line brought into the new line the following vessels: the partly constructed *Queen Mary*, *Berengaria*, *Aquitania*, *Mauretania*, *Scythia*, *Samaria*, *Carinthia*, *Franconia*, *Laconia*, *Ausonia*, *Antonia*, *Aurania*, *Andania*, *Ascania*.

The White Star Line the *Majestic*, *Olympic*, *Homeric*, *Britannic*, *Georgic*, *Doric* and *Laurentic*.

Since the merger took place the *Olympic*, *Majestic*, *Homeric*, *Mauretania* and *Doric* have been scrapped and the *Laurentic* has been withdrawn from service.

HISTORIES OF SOME FAMOUS BRITISH SHIPPING LINES

THE CUNARD LINE

This historic line, whose history is the history of steam navigation, was founded in 1839 by Samuel Cunard in association with Mr. George Burns and Mr. David McIvor, two of the ablest shipping men in Great Britain.

Samuel Cunard, who was later knighted by H.M. Queen Victoria, was of Canadian birth and origin, his native city being Halifax, Nova Scotia.

The partners entered into an agreement with the British Government to commence a monthly mail service, with steamships, between Liverpool–Halifax and Boston. The Company was named the British and North American Royal Mail Steamships Company. Ordering four steamers of just over 1,100 tons each, the first sailing being the *Britannia* on July 4th, 1840, *Britannia's* three sisters being named *Acadia*, *Caledonia* and *Columbia*. All four were wooden hulled paddle steamers with simple side lever type engines of about 740 indicated horse power, designed by that famous engineer, Mr. Robert Napier.

Following these first steamers a number of similar vessels were added to the fleet of gradually increasing size, until in 1856 the first Cunard iron hulled steamer, *Persia*, was built. The *Scotia* of 1862, with a tonnage of 3,871 tons, was the largest steamer in the world: the *Gallia* of 1879, 4,800 tons, regarded as the grand-parent of the modern liner; the *Servia* of 1881, 7,392 tons, was the first steel vessel of the line and larger and faster than any steamship then in commission, and the *Aurania* of 1883, 13,360 tons, was the first liner to be fitted with suites of rooms.

Of course many other vessels besides the foregoing were built both for the main route and for other services which the Company ran at different times in its career. For instance, in the year 1850 the Cunard Company, as it had generally become known, owned seventeen steamships with a capital value of something like £1,500,000. The Company then being a private one did not publish balance sheets but the above approximate figure can be taken on the authority of the *Liverpool Albion* of February 2nd, 1852.

In 1878 the line was turned into a private limited company named The Cunard Steamship Company, Ltd., with a capital of £2,000,000 in 20,000 shares. This was made a public company in 1880.

The year 1884 was notable in the history of the Company by the inception of the two record-making express mail steamers, *Umbria* and *Etruria*, each of over 8,000 tons gross. Within a short time these vessels broke all existing speed records and became the most popular vessels on the Atlantic.

After another decade had passed these notable vessels were in turn eclipsed by the commissioning of the first Cunard twin-screw steamers *Campania* and *Lucania* of 1893 of approximately 12,000 tons, and with a speed of 22 knots, which made them the ships of the day. *Lucania* came to an untimely end by being practically destroyed by fire and sunk in Huskisson Dock, Liverpool, in the year 1909. In 1901 this vessel was the first Atlantic liner to be fitted with wireless. The *Campania* survived to the end of the Great War, when she was lost while serving as an aeroplane carrier in the Firth of Forth.

The year 1905 marked a further development in the Company's North Atlantic service by the building of the two famous 20,000 tonners *Carmania* and *Caronia*.

They were followed in 1905 by the two most famous ships ever known on the Atlantic, the *Lusitania* and *Mauretania*; these great ships, records in both size and speed, brought back to Britain the coveted Blue Riband of the Atlantic, which incidentally the Cunard Line has held during the ninety-four years between 1840 and 1934 for over half that period.

The next great milestone in the history of the Company was the commissioning in 1913 of the great *Aquitania*, the last pre-war vessel of the line.

During the war the Company lost 56 per cent of the fleet, and throughout the four years, 1914–18, Cunard ships transported over 1,000,000 troops, 10,000,000 tons of foodstuffs, and over 100,000 tons of fuel oil for the British Navy.

After the war the Cunard Company acquired the *Berengaria*, which took her place on the Southampton–New York service with the *Aquitania* and *Mauretania*. The Company in 1919 changing the terminal port for the express mail service from Liverpool to Southampton.

The Company, to replace their war losses, ordered no less than thirteen new steamships, totalling 214,000 tons.

THE WHITE STAR LINE

The White Star Line or the Oceanic Steam Navigation Company, Ltd., to give its official title, was founded in 1869 by the late Mr. Thomas Henry Ismay, whose career was one of the romances of the shipping trade in the latter half of the nineteenth century. Coming to Liverpool from Cumberland he served his apprenticeship with the well-known firm of Imrie, Tomlinson and Company, after which he commenced business as a shipbroker.

Although at the time there were five or six steamship companies engaged in the Liverpool–New York passenger trade, Mr. Ismay felt that there was room for another, and such was the trust in the powers of this young man of thirty-two years that the capital of £750,000 in £1,000 shares was rapidly subscribed.

He had previously purchased the White Star house-flag from a Liverpool firm of sailing ship owners, and the first steamer of the new line and the first steamer to fly the pennant that nowadays is familiar on all the Seven Seas was the pioneer *Oceanic*, an iron, single screw steamer of 3,897 tons gross, built by Messrs. Harland & Wolff, Ltd., at Belfast.

The *Oceanic* left Liverpool on her maiden voyage on March 2nd, 1871, and was the first liner to have the dining saloon and staterooms placed amidships, and the provision of separate chairs in the dining saloon.

She was followed by a number of ships of increasing tonnage, when in 1874–5 the fine 5,000 ton single screw steamers, *Britannic* and *Germanic* were built; these steamers cut the Liverpool–New York passage to 7½ days.

Then in 1889–90 the advent of the speedy *Teutonic* and *Majestic* again lowered the Atlantic record. Following these came the second *Oceanic*, a great ship of 17,000 tons and the first to exceed in length the famous *Great Eastern*. Mr. T. H. Ismay died in November, 1899, only two months after his latest and greatest vessel had commenced her maiden voyage.

Between 1901 and 1908 the famous "White Star Big Four" were built ranging from *Celtic*, 21,000 tons, to *Adriatic* of 25,000 tons.

In 1902 the Company became part of the International Mercantile Marine Company, the shipping trust as it was generally known.

The Company in 1909 entered the Canadian trade in conjunction with the Dominion Line, and also in conjunction with the Shaw, Savill & Albion Company was in the Australian and New Zealand trade.

In 1911 and 1912 the line built the two largest ships as yet to be built, *Olympic* and *Titanic*, the latter unfortunately never completing her maiden voyage; she was replaced in 1914 by the *Britannic*, which was never destined to steam in the service of her owners.

Since the War many other fine liners were either built or acquired, the largest being the great *Majestic*.

The Company changed its terminal port for the express service from Liverpool to Southampton about 1911, keeping an intermediate service going from Liverpool.

About the year 1920 the Royal Mail Steam Packet Company, which had commenced a service to New York, entered into negotiations for the purchase of the White Star Line from the International Mercantile Marine Company and eventually this deal was carried through.

The last vessels built by the line before the merger with the Cunard Line was the splendid motor vessels *Britannic* and *Georgic*.

THE CUNARD STEAMSHIP COMPANY, LIMITED

Chairman: Sir Percy Bates.
Issued capital, £8,070,261.   Debenture stock issued, £4,592,518.
Book value of properties, investments and fleet, £14,287,234.

This Company besides owning the larger interest in the Cunard White Star Line still operates a fleet of steamers on the Liverpool–Mediterranean Sea service as well as owning interests in other shipping companies, prominently amongst which is the Commonwealth and Dominion Line, Ltd., known as the "Port Line," which runs a fleet of twenty-six modern cargo liners between London and New Zealand and Australia, and between New Zealand, Australia and New York. The fleet includes many recently built motor ships of between 8,000 and 9,000 tons gross, the latest being the m.s. *Port Wyndham*, 8,580 tons gross and the m.s. *Port Townsville*, 8,650 tons gross. All the ships are named after ports in Australia and New Zealand.

The Commonwealth and Dominion Line was established in 1913 to take over the fleets and interests of the Tyser Line, Roydens Indra Line, Corry's Belfast Star Line and Milburn & Company, who were established in 1869. In 1916 Sir Thomas Royden, Chairman of the Cunard S.S. Company, and who was also Chairman of the Commonwealth Dominion Line, arranged the absorption of the latter line by the Cunard Company.

HISTORIES OF SOME FAMOUS BRITISH SHIPPING LINES

THE P. & O. STEAM NAVIGATION, COMPANY, LONDON

Present fleet, 41 steamships.   Approximate total gross tonnage, 433,000.

Present Chairman of Board of Directors, The Hon. Alex. Shaw.

This Company, one of the oldest steamship companies in the world, now controls the largest group of shipping companies in existence. Founded in 1836 as the Peninsular Steam Navigation Company, to run a steamer service to Spain and Portugal, later extending its services to the Mediterranean seaports. The Company obtained the contract for the Indian mails in 1842, the first mail steamer was the *Hindustan*, the mails being carried by sea to Alexandria from whence they travelled overland to Port Said. There steamers sent round the Cape of Good Hope from England, picked up the mails and took them on to Bombay. The first steamer of the Company was the *Iberia*, which sailed in 1837 from London.

With the opening of the Suez Canal in 1869 a through service was established from England to India for mails and passengers instead of the longer route via the Cape or the broken route via Alexandria.

Gradually the services were increased and extended to China, Japan and Australia.

In 1910 the Company bought Lund's Blue Anchor Line, with service to Australia via the Cape, and continued the service as the P. & O. Branch Line.

The Company with its subsidiaries and associated companies now control steamship services encircling the entire world.

In 1929 the Company was the first British or European Line to adopt turbo-electric drive for a big passenger liner, the first liner being the famous luxurious Indian mail steamship the *Viceroy of India*.

The history of the company is the history of steam navigation in the near and far eastern waters.

The late Lord Inchcape, the Chairman of the Company, who died in 1932, had been largely responsible for building up the Company and group to its present great position and his death was a great loss to the Company and to the shipping world. The principle vessels of the fleet are:

Strathmore	.	1935	23,500 tons gr.	*Comorin*	. .	1925	15,241 tons gr.
Strathnaver	.	1931	22,283 ,, ,,	*Chitral*	. .	1925	15,346 ,, ,,
Strathaird	.	1932	22,284 ,, ,,	*Cathay*	. .	1925	15,225 ,, ,,
Viceroy of India	.	1929	19,627 ,, ,,	*Mongolia*	. .	1923	16,600 ,, ,,
Mooltan	.	1923	20,952 ,, ,,	*Moldavia*	. .	1922	16,556 ,, ,,
Maloja	.	1923	20,014 ,, ,,	*Narkunda*	.	1920	16,632 ,, ,,
Rajputana	.	1926	16,664 ,, ,,	*Naldera*	. .	1918	16,113 ,, ,,
Ranchi	.	1925	16,738 ,, ,,	*Corfu*	. .	1931	14,170 ,, ,,
Rawalpindi	.	1925	16,697 ,, ,,	*Carthage*	. .	1931	14,182 ,, ,,
Ranpura	.	1925	16,688 ,, ,,				

THE NEW ZEALAND SHIPPING COMPANY

This Company is also in the group. With its subsidiary company, the Federal Steam Navigation Company, has a fine fleet.

Combined fleets, 30 vessels.   Approximate tonnage, 370,000 tons. gross

The New Zealand Shipping Company was founded in the year 1873 at Christchurch, New Zealand, with a number of sailing vessels. The first mail steamer being the *British King* of 1883. The present fleets being:

NEW ZEALAND SHIPPING CO.				FEDERAL STEAM NAVIGATION CO.			
M.S. *Rangitane*	.	1929	16,712 tons gr.	M.S. *Durham*	.	1934	10,893 tons gr.
M.T. *Rangitata*	.	1929	16,737 ,, ,,	M.S. *Dorset*	.	1935	10,893 ,, ,,
M.S. *Rangitiki*	.	1929	16,698 ,, ,,	*Northumberland*	.	1915	11,555 ,, ,,
Remuera	. .	1911	11,383 ,, ,,	*Norfolk*	.	1918	10,948 ,, ,,
Rotorua	. .	1911	10,890 ,, ,,	*Huntington*	.	1920	10,946 ,, ,,
Ruahine	. .	1909	10,870 ,, ,,	*Cumberland*	.	1919	10,937 ,, ,,
M.S. *Otaio*	.	1930	10,048 ,, ,,	*Hertford*	.	1917	10,603 ,, ,,
M.S. *Orari*	.	1931	10,350 ,, ,,	*Cornwall*	.	1920	10,603 ,, ,,
M.S. *Opawa*	.	1931	10,107 ,, ,,	*Cambridge*	.	1916	10,846 ,, ,,
Hurunui	.	1920	9,315 ,, ,,	*Westmorland*	.	1917	8,999 ,, ,,
Hororata	.	1914	9,178 ,, ,,	*Middlesex*	.	1920	8,703 ,, ,,
Tasmania	.	1913	9,008 ,, ,,	*Somerset*	.	1918	8,569 ,, ,,
Tongariro	.	1925	8,719 ,, ,,	*Surrey*	.	1919	8,564 ,, ,,
Tirakina		1923	8,706 ,, ,,	*Kent*	.	1918	8,694 ,, ,,
Tekoa	.	1922	8,689 ,, ,,	M.S. *Essex*	.	1936	—
Piako	.	1920	8,283 ,, ,,	M.S. *Sussex*	.	1936	—

ORIENT LINE

Present fleet 7 steamers.   Approximate total tonnage, 150,267 tons gross.

An important line which, while under entirely separate ownership and management, is closely associated with the P. & O. group, is the Orient Line, a line famous in the London–Australian trade since the days of sailing ships.

As far back as 1853, if not earlier, there was an Orient Line of clipper ships to Australia, the owners of this line being James Thomson & Company, a firm founded in 1797. In 1863 the style of the firm was changed to Anderson, Thomson & Company, and in 1870 to Anderson, Anderson & Company. The most famous of the clipper ships was the *Orient*, 1,032 tons, built on the River Thames at Nelson Dock, Rotherhithe.

In the late 1870's the Orient Company began a 14-day service of mail steamers to Australia from London, in association with the Pacific Steam Navigation Company, from whom the earliest steamers were purchased.

In those days the fleet was composed of ships which must seem very small to modern eyes—the *Lusitania*, *Garonne*, *Chimborazo* and the *Cuzco*, all under 4,000 tons, the *Orient*, 5,386 tons, the *Ormuz*, 6,031 tons, and the *Austral*, 5,588 tons.

The *Orient*, which reached London from the builders in 1879, was one of the wonders of the world at the time. When launched, she was the largest steamer in the world excepting the *Great Eastern*. She was the first steamer to have a promenade deck. Her voyages continued for many years with great regularity, and instead of her owners disposing of her for breaking up purposes, the *Orient* was given a new lease of life and received new engines and boilers. Her internal arrangements were also improved and brought up to date. When she reappeared in Australia her identity was entirely changed, for she had only one tall funnel and two masts, so different from when she first voyaged to that continent. She made a number of voyages until newer and faster vessels were added to the fleet; in 1900 she was disposed of for £12,000 to Italian owners and was not again seen in the Australian trade.

The year 1889 marks an interesting development of Orient, and indeed of shipping history, for in that year the *Chimborazo* and *Garonne* were despatched on cruises to the Norwegian Fjords. From this small beginning the cruising business, which employs so many ships of all nations and seamen to-day, has helped so enormously to encourage the growth of sea travel.

The *Ophir*, a 7,000 ton vessel completed in 1891, was the first twin screw passenger ship to go east of Suez and marked a great advance in liner construction. She possessed an exceptional turn of speed, and was lavishly decorated and furnished. In fact she rather resembled a great yacht; a ship of many virtues but with one serious defect—she was exceedingly costly to run, and, roughly speaking, the more voyages she made the more money she lost. Her true metier was found in 1901, when she was commissioned by the Admiralty to carry the Duke and Duchess of York (the late King George V and Queen Mary) to Australia, where they opened the Commonwealth Parliament, and afterwards on their tour to New Zealand, South Africa and Canada.

New additions to the fleet gradually increased in size—the *Omrah* of 1899, 8,291 tons, and the *Orontes* of 1902, 9,023 tons.

A turning point in the Company's fortunes was reached in 1907; then the Royal Mail Steam Packet Company, who had a year or two before bought the Pacific Steam Navigation Company, terminated the working arrangement between the Orient Line and the Pacific Steam Navigation Company. With its own ships alone the Orient Line could not possibly maintain the 14-day service which had been provided for the previous thirty years. Six new steamers of 12,000 tons each were ordered and delivered during the next three years, to implement the Australian mail contract—no small venture for a company which had so small a capital as the Orient Steam Navigation Company then possessed. These were the *Orsova*, *Osterley*, *Otway*, *Otranto*, *Orvieto* and *Orama*, and they were such fine vessels that the Orient Line reaped a reward commensurate with their enterprise during the first few years of their life.

The 14-day sailings were maintained uninterruptedly until the outbreak of the Great War in 1914, when the requisitioning of steamers by the British Government broke the continuity of sailings.

In August, 1914, the Line possessed nine fine ships, the smallest being the *Ophir* and the largest and latest, the *Orama* of 12,927 tons. During the war, in 1917, a still larger ship was completed, the *Ormonde*, of 15,000 tons. In addition, the *Huntsgreen*, late the German liner *Derfflinger*, which had been seized in Egypt, was managed for the British Shipping Controller by the line.   Between them these eleven ships carried three quarters of a million troops, besides performing numerous other duties.   Four were lost, a fifth was torpedoed but was beached and later repaired and restored to service.

The most famous of them all was the *Otranto*, which was attached to Admiral Cradock's ill-fated squadron, and was fortunate in escaping from the disastrous action at Coronel.   Later she was converted to a troopship, and in this service sank after collision in a storm with another transport.   Four hundred American troops were lost with her, but as many more were saved by a courageous destroyer captain, who time after time took his tiny craft alongside the sinking vessel in a gale.

The *Otway* was torpedoed and sunk after two and a half years' service as an armed merchant cruiser.   Like the *Otranto*, the *Orama* was commissioned as an auxiliary cruiser and helped in the rounding up of the *Dresden*, the last survivor of Admiral Von Spee's fleet.   For more than two years after that she served as an auxiliary cruiser, and was torpedoed in 1917.   The *Omrah* was torpedoed in 1918, whilst serving as a troopship.

Thus at the end of the war, the fleet was sadly reduced.   Four ships had been lost and the oldest of the Company's vessels, the *Ophir*, had been purchased by the British Government.   To enable the Company to carry on, three ex-German liners were bought from the Shipping Controller—the *Zeppelin*, *Prinz Ludwig* and *Konigin Louise*, renamed *Ormuz*, *Orcades* and *Omar*.   Gradually the mail and passenger service was resumed, though for some months the repatriation of Australian troops was the first concern of the fleet.   Modern vessels were badly needed but the post-war boom made building prices prohibitive and the construction of new ships was postponed until 1924, when the first of the five fine 20,000 ton liners added between 1924 and 1929 was launched.

The new ships—*Orama*, *Oronsay*, *Otranto*, *Orford* and *Orontes* (all detailed in this book) came just in time for the post-war rush of emigration.   This faded away to nothing in 1930; surplus tonnage was promptly scrapped and the *Ormuz* was sold to her former owners, the North German Lloyd Company, who renamed her *Dresden*, and she was lost by going ashore on a cruise to the Norwegian Fjords not very long afterwards.

In December, 1933, a new vessel, the *Orion*, of 23,370 tons, was ordered from Messrs. Vickers Armstrong, Ltd.   She was completed in 1935.   At the end of 1935 a sister ship to the *Orion* was ordered from the same builders, and is to be named *Orcades*.

The present fleet is:

Orion	.	. 1935	23,371 tons gr.	Oronsay	.	. 1925	20,001 tons gr.
Orontes	.	. 1929	19,970 ,, ,,	Orama	.	. 1924	19,819 ,, ,,
Orford	.	. 1929	19,942 ,, ,,	Ormonde	.	. 1917	14,982 ,, ,,
Otranto	.	. 1925	20,032 ,, ,,				

The next important company in the group is the great

BRITISH INDIA STEAM NAVIGATION COMPANY

Present fleet, 112 steam and motor   Approximate total tons gross 671,593.
ships.
Present Chairman of Company, the Hon. Alex. Shaw.

The Company was founded in the year 1855, when the late Sir William
MacKinnon established the Calcutta & Burmah Steam Navigation Company
to operate mail services on the Indian coast, the first steamers being the *Cape
of Good Hope* and *Baltic* sent out from England in 1857.   In 1869 on the opening
of the Suez Canal the Company's steamer *India* carried the first cargo of Indian
produce through the Canal.   The line operates services from England to Egypt,
Arabia, Persia, India, Burmah, East Indies, Zanzibar, East Africa, South Africa,
with many inter-colonial routes from India to Australia and Africa, South and
East Africa to Australia, etc.

The Duke of Windsor, when H.R.H. The Prince of Wales, travelled in one of
the Company's mail steamers when he visited East Africa.

The largest vessels in the fleet are *Dilwara*, 1935, 11,000 tons gross; *Talma*,
1923, 10,000 tons gross; *Tilawa*, 1924, 10,006 tons gross; *Mulbera*, 1922, 9,100,
tons gross; *Modasa*, 1921, 9,070 tons gross; *Mantola*, 1921, 9,064 tons gross;
Malda, 1922, 9,066 tons gross; *Matiana*, 1922, 9,045 tons gross; *Madura*, 1921,
9,032 tons gross; M.S. *Domala*, 1921, 8,441 tons gross; M.S. *Dumana*, 1923, 8,427
tons gross.

THE ROYAL MAIL LINES, LTD.

The successors of the Royal Mail Steam Packet Company.

Present fleet, 36 motor and steam-   Approximate total tonnage, 322,100.
ships.

The present Company was formed in 1932 to take over the South American
interests of the Royal Mail Steam Packet Company and the Nelson Line.   The
R.M.S.P. Co. was founded in 1839 and incorporated by Royal Charter to
establish a service to the British West Indies.   This Company acquired many
interests in other companies under the management of Sir Alfred Jones, and latterly
under the control of Lord Kylsant, it became the principal company in the largest
group of shipping companies ever known, including the Pacific Steam Navigation
Company, which was one of its first acquisitions, the Nelson Line, the White Star
Line, Shaw, Savill & Albion Line, the Aberdeen White Star line, Union Castle
Line, Elder Dempster Line, Coast Line, and many other passenger and cargo
lines.

These lines have now been either split into groups or sold outright and the
present Royal Mail Lines, Ltd., includes the fleets of the R.M.S.P. Co. and the
Nelson Line and works in close association with the Pacific Steam Navigation
Company.

The largest vessels of the fleet are:

		tons gr.			tons gr.
s.s. *Alcantara* . .	1926	22,200	M.S. *Highland Monarch* .	1928	14,137
s.s. *Almanzora* . .	1914	15,551	M.S. *Highland Princess* .	1929	14,128
s.s. *Atlantis* . . .	1913	15,135	M.S. *Highland Patriot* .	1932	14,157
s.s. *Asturias* . . .	1925	22,048	M.S. *Highland Brigade* .	1929	14,131
s.s. *Arlanza* . : .	1912	14,622	M.S. *Highland Chieftain* .	1929	14,131

The last five motor ships originally being the fleet of the Nelson Line.

THE UNION-CASTLE MAIL STEAMSHIP COMPANY, LTD.

Chairman: Mr. Robertson F. Gibbs.

Present fleet, 29 vessels.   Approximate total tonnage, 365,000 tons gross.

This important line was formed in 1900 by the amalgamation of two rival companies engaged in the South African trade, named the Union Steamship Company, which was established in 1853, and the Castle Line founded by the late Sir Donald Currie in 1862, who brought about the union of the two competitors.

After the death of Sir Donald Currie the line came under the control of the Royal Mail Steam Packet Company, but retained its own individuality and management. The Company also owns an interest in the Natal Line, Messrs. Bullard King & Company, Ltd., which also operates a service between London and South Africa.

The mail and passenger service of the line is Southampton to Capetown via Madeira and Canary Islands, with an intermediate service from London to Capetown, Durban, Beira and Mauritius, etc., and other service from London to South and East Africa via the Suez Canal, also between South Africa and New York.

The main units of the present fleet are:

		tons gr.			tons gr.
M.S. *Athlone Castle* . .	1936	25,000	s.s. *Balmoral Castle* . .	1910	13,336
s.s. *Stirling Castle* . .	1935	25,000	M.S. *Dunnottar Castle* .	1936	15,000
M.S. *Warwick Castle* . .	1930	20,445	M.S. *Dunvegan Castle* . .	1936	15,000
M.S. *Winchester Castle* .	1930	20,109	M.S. *Llangibby Castle* .	1929	11,951
M.S. *Carnarvon Castle* .	1926	20,063	M.S. *Dunbar Castle* . .	1930	10,002
s.s. *Windsor Castle* . .	1922	18,973	M.S. *Rothesay Castle* .	1935	7,000
s.s. *Arundel Castle* . .	1921	19,029	M.S. *Roslin Castle* . .	1935	7,025
s.s. *Edinburgh Castle* .	1910	13,330			